"Comforted of God"

Compiled by Algernon J Pollock

Scripture Truth Publications

"COMFORTED OF GOD"

First edition published by R.Besley, London.
Second edition published by Dible & Besley, London.
Third edition published c1910 by The Central Bible Truth Depôt, 12 Paternoster Row, London, E.C.
Fourth edition published c1916 (19th thousand) by The Central Bible Truth Depôt, 12 Paternoster Row, London, E.C.
Fifth edition published c1921 (24th thousand) by The Central Bible Truth Depôt, 5 Rose Street, Paternoster Square, London, E.C.4.
Sixth edition published c1937 (29th thousand) by The Central Bible Truth Depôt, 5 Rose Street, Paternoster Square, London, E.C.
Seventh edition published c1948 (31st thousand) by The Central Bible Truth Depôt, 11 Little Britain, London, E.C.1
First abridged edition published c1965 by The Central Bible Truth Depôt, 11 Little Britain, London, E.C.1

Eighth Edition April 2010
Re-typeset and transferred to Digital Printing 2010
ISBN: 978-0-901860-63-7 (paperback)
© Copyright 2010 Scripture Truth

All rights reserved. No part of this publication may be reproduced, stored in a retrieval system, or transmitted, in any form or by any means, electronic, mechanical, photocopying, recording or otherwise without prior permission of Scripture Truth Publications.

Scripture quotations are taken from The Authorized (King James) Version. Rights in the Authorized Version are vested in the Crown. Reproduced by permission of the Crown's patentee, Cambridge University Press.

Cover photograph ©iStockphoto.com/ratluk

Published by Scripture Truth Publications
31-33 Glover Street, Crewe, Cheshire, CW1 3LD
Scripture Truth is an imprint of Central Bible Hammond Trust, a charitable trust
Typesetting by John Rice
Printed and bound by Lightning Source

"COMFORTED OF GOD"

Introduction

This little book, originally compiled before the First World War, shines the light of God's Word into the dark situations of disappointment, illness and bereavement. In such circumstances it provides encouragement, strength, illumination, understanding and comfort. Over thirty thousand copies were produced during the first half of the twentieth century, bringing relief to many.

Over one hundred years have passed since the first edition was compiled, and yet the basic problems of the human condition remain essentially unchanged; and God's Word has as much to say to those facing the darkest of situations in the twenty-first century as it ever did.

I have personally derived great encouragement from dipping into this book in times of personal stress, and reading it again as it was prepared for re-publication only served to confirm its immensely valuable role in using prose and poetry to lift the spirit and draw the stressed, the discouraged and the sorrowful to the Saviour, who is the Prince of Peace.

John Rice
April 2010

"*BLESSED be God, even the Father of our Lord Jesus Christ, THE FATHER OF MERCIES, AND THE GOD OF ALL COMFORT*; who comforteth us in all our tribulation, that we may be able to comfort them which are in any trouble, by the comfort wherewith we ourselves are **comforted of God.**"

2 Corinthians 1:3-4.

*   *   *   *

"If any little word of mine
  Can make a life the brighter;
If any little song of mine
  Can make a heart the lighter,
God help me speak that little word,
  And take my life of singing,
And drop it in some lonely vale,
  To set the echoes ringing."

CONTENTS

A Bright Prospect 63
A Commonplace Life (*poem*) 24
A Few Thoughts on Psalm 23 and John 10 80
A Good Answer 15
A Letter 95
A Letter to One Bereaved 13
A Psalm of Silence (*poem*) 94
A Word to Doubters (*poem*) 86
"Abba, Father" (*poem*) 54

"Be Still!" (*poem*) 45
"Bringing into Captivity every Thought" 27
"But He giveth *more* grace" 105

Cleave to the Lord 91
Comfort in Sorrow (*poem*) 23
"Comforted of God" (*poem*) 9
Counting on God for everything 37

Everlasting Love 89
Extracts 70

"Fear Not" (*poem*) 88
Fragments 4, 22, 34, 109

God is Better than our *Faith* 27
God Knows Best (*poem*) 86
God ... the Great Deliverer 107

"He knoweth them that trust in Him" 25
His Appointment (*poem*) 80

I Know Not! (*poem*) 40
In the Hand of God (*poem*) 76
In the Plains of Jordan (*poem*) 58
In Time of Trouble 22

"Jesus Christ, the same Yesterday and To-day and for Ever" 31

Last Words of Samuel Rutherford (*poem*) 98
Lean and Pray (*poem*) 41
Little Tangles 104
Look Up! (*poem*) 19

Manna by the Way 44
"Meditate upon these things" 68
"My cup runneth over" 18

"Not Now" (*poem*) 30
Nothing to do with To-morrow (*poem*) 12
Now and Hereafter 77
Numbers 6:24 (*poem*) 12

Oil and Wine (*poem*) 53
On Prayer 61

Paul Gerhardt alone with God 38
Peace 103
Peerless Worth (*poem*) 36
"Perfect through Suffering" 10
Perfect through Suffering (*poem*) 35
Psalm 23 20

"Rest at Noon" 96

Samuel Rutherford's Dying Testimony 62
Settled Peace 81
Simply Clinging 109
Sometime, Somewhere (*poem*) 71
"Step by Step" 93
Stray Thoughts 43
Strength in Looking Up 24
Stripped but Blessed 48

"Take heed unto thyself" 64
"Take ... no Thought for the Morrow" 66
Texts 4, 21, 67
The Burden-Bearer 15
The Burden of Prayer (*poem*) 88
"The Father's Care" (*poem*) 53

"COMFORTED OF GOD"

"The Garment of Praise for the Spirit of Heaviness" .. 55
The Glory of that Light (*poem*) 84
"The Light that Failed" 75
The Lord of Hosts and the God of Jacob 72
The Peacock's Feathers 32
The Permanent and the Passing Away 90
The Pilgrim (*poem*) 16
The Power of the Cross of Christ 83
The Tapestry Weavers (*poem*) 47
The Touch of Jesus (*poem*) 81
The Truest Comfort in Sorrow 28
The Way Home (*poem*) 52
"Thou hast made me exceeding glad with
    Thy countenance" (*poem*) 42
Thou Knowest (*poem*) 76
Three Needles 60
"Thy faithfulness reacheth unto the clouds" (*poem*) ... 41
Thy Saviour loves thee (*poem*) 59

Unveiled Mysteries 87

"What will it be?" (*poem*) 46
"Who shall roll away the Stone?" (*poem*) 82

7

"COMFORTED OF GOD"

"Comforted of God"

GOD must acquaint His comforters with grief,
  Else have their words the tinkling cymbal sound;
He first who brought the wounded heart relief,
  Himself lay stricken, bleeding on the ground.
The eagle, mounting high with sunlit wings,
Fears not the random dart the heedless marksman flings.

Oh! there is truth surpassing mortal ken,
  That God, through suffering, teacheth to His own;
Yea, glories unperceived by faithless men,
  Too vast for Faith herself to view alone,
Thrice happy who, in frequent tears and pain
Those blissful heights, step after step, with Him may gain.

Why should this human heart, instinct with love,
  Expect an answer in the stranger-land?
Enough to have a full response above;
  Enough that One its way can understand.
Let love on earth her wealth in streamlets spend;
Its *depths* are all reserved for one Celestial Friend.

"Perfect through Suffering"

Written by one laid for years on a couch of suffering

I KEPT, for nearly a year, the flask-shaped cocoon of an Emperor moth. It is very peculiar in its construction. A narrow opening is left in the neck of the flask, through which the perfect insect forces its way, so that a forsaken cocoon is as entire as one still tenanted, no rupture of the interlacing fibres having taken place.

The great disproportion between the means of egress and the size of the prisoned insect makes one wonder how the exit is ever accomplished at all, and it never is without great labour and difficulty. It is supposed that the pressure to which the moth's body is subjected in passing through the narrow opening is a provision of nature for forcing the juices into vessels of the wings, these being less developed at the period of emergence from the chrysalis than they are in other insects.

I happened to witness the first efforts of my imprisoned moth to escape from its long confinement. Nearly a whole forenoon, from time to time, I watched it patiently striving and struggling to get out. It never seemed able to get beyond a certain point, and at last my patience was exhausted. I thought I was wiser and more compassionate than its Maker, and resolved to give it a helping hand.

With the points of my scissors I snipped the confining threads to make the exit just a *very little* easier, and lo! immediately, and with perfect ease, out crawled my moth, dragging a swollen body, and little shrivelled wings. In vain I watched to see that marvellous progress of expansion in which the wings silently and swiftly develop before our eyes, and as I traced the exquisite spots and working of divers colours which were all there in *miniature*, I longed to see these assume their due proportions, and the creature appear in all its perfect beauty, as in truth it is one of the loveliest of its kind.

But I looked in vain; my false tenderness had proved its ruin. It never was anything but a stunted abortion, crawling painfully through that brief life which it should have spent flying the air on rainbow wings.

The lesson I got that day has often stood me in good stead. It has helped me to understand what has been called "the *hardness* of God's love." I have thought of it often when watching with pitiful eyes those who were struggling with sorrows, suffering, or distress, and it has seemed to me that I was more merciful than God, and I would fain have cut short the discipline, and given deliverance. Short-sighted fool! how know I that one of those pains and groans could be spared? The far-sighted, perfect love of God, which seeks the perfection of its object, does not weakly shrink from present transient suffering. Our Father's love is too true to be weak. Because He loves His children He chastens them, that they may be "partakers of His holiness". With this glorious end in view, He spares not for their crying. "Made perfect *through* suffering," as Christ was, the sons of God are trained up to obedience, and brought to glory "*through* much tribulation."

* * * *

"I would HASTEN my escape." (*Psalm 55:8*).

"All the days of my appointed time will I WAIT." (*Job 14:14*).

Numbers 6:24

"The Lord Bless Thee!"

How shall He bless thee?
With the gladness that knoweth no decay,
With the riches that cannot pass away,
With the sunshine that makes an endless day—
Thus may He bless thee!

"And Keep Thee!"

How shall He keep thee?
With the all-covering shadow of His wings,
With the strong love that guards from evil things,
With the sure power that safe to glory brings—
Thus may He keep thee!

NOTHING TO DO WITH TO-MORROW

I HAVE nothing to do with to-morrow,
  My Father will make that His care,
Should He fill it with trouble and sorrow,
  He'll help me that sorrow to bear.

I have nothing to do with to-morrow,
  Its troubles then why should I share,
Its grace and its strength I can't borrow,
  Then why should I borrow its care?

A Letter to One Bereaved

ONE of the leading effects of sorrow and bereavement is to cast a veil over things present, and to bring us into the presence of God and eternal things in heaven. The result of this is that we are astonished to find how strange we are to the things of God and of heaven. To know what faith in Christ secures to us, and to be practically in the familiar use of it, are two very distinguishable things. I know that faith in Christ makes me His for eternity, and makes His Father to be my Father, and the Spirit to be Comforter to me. It gives me eternity and heaven, and cuts me off from earth. But, alas! the being so blessed, and the being able to act upon it, are two very different things, more so than having learnt a language theoretically and thoroughly, and being able to speak it.

Now when sorrow and bereavement come, things present for the time fade, and things heavenly and eternal assume more substance to our minds. The object of your love gone to heaven and God and Christ. There is a void down here. The place that was ever full of refreshing water is dried up. **You are left**, and your mind in grace follows the one you love upward. But, then, perhaps you find how little you know of the God he has gone to, of the Saviour who is there, of his present state, of the connection of the pool down here, and the grace that gave it to you, and the present bereavement of his presence in the pure light above, and of the restoration in the end to God's glory and his own profit.

How often have I learnt in such a season that I had not been living to the glory of God; that lo, I come to do Thy will, to suffer Thy will, had not been my principle of conduct; and God in such hours has seemed a strange God, a God I had neglected, and practically been living without. **Self-ignorance**, too, giving Satan power against us at such seasons; for, if we do not attribute to our own sin the having been living practically so far from God, not to be **at home with His ways of dealing** and with **Himself**, Satan will boldly inspire not only hard thoughts of God, but hard words against Him too.

Now, it is clear that God is perfect in wisdom, love, power and goodness. It is only because I, His child, am not in the light of His plans and wisdom, that I think I could have done better for myself than He has done. He gave me a pool, and I thought more of its suitability to myself and others than of Him who gave it, and when He took it away, then I found that I had not been thinking of Himself, but of His gifts, like Job. Poor Job; self-ignorance led him to mistake God for Satan and Satan for God! I have known this lesson too, and how, if I did not see the hardness of my own heart, **God seemed hard**; and how, if I had been living at a distance from God and did not confess it, God seemed at a distance; and how, if I did not confess that the selfishness of fallen humanity had led me, a saint, to walk as if there were a veil between God and me down here, I felt as if the heavens were brass, and that He made it so. I had not leaned upon the arm of God, and to confess this according to the Spirit, or to leave Satan to suggest that God's arm was raised against me was the alternative; to confess that I had forgotten God, or that God had forgotten me.

But then, it is love divine which, having made us to be everything to Christ, insists upon teaching us now to make Christ **everything** to ourselves down here. The jealousy of His love, who as the Father, is not satisfied that we take or have anything but Christ as the portion of our souls or our joy, and the jealousy of Christ's heart cannot be satisfied that we should have anything but His Father as our choice. These lessons break us, and let God and Christ into our souls and make us feel our need of them.

The Burden-Bearer

SOMEWHERE I read a parable, the exact details of which have faded from my memory. At the time of reading it, a deep impression was made on my mind, and its main thought I have often recalled with delight and refreshment.

The parable ran like this. A man had a vision in which he saw a multitude of people bearing burdens, which greatly afflicted him to behold. Strong men were bowed down under heavy loads, fragile women were staggering under burdens, even children were weighed down. All classes of people were represented, toiling and staggering under heavy burdens.

In the vision the dreamer thought he saw the Lord, and to his utter amazement He was busily employed in increasing the burdens. Still the burdened ones toiled on, ready to drop—but not quite. Still the Lord added to their burdens again and again, till at last the man's curiosity and surprise could be restrained no longer.

He enquired of the Lord why He was adding to the burdens and distresses of those he saw. The reply was:—

"I am adding to their burdens till they cannot do without Me any longer, and *then I will carry both them and their burdens."*

A Good Answer

WHEN surprise was expressed at the patience of a poor Arab woman under heavy affliction, she said: "When we look at God's face, we do not feel His hand." Can you not go a good step further, you who know a Saviour-God as Father, and substitute a Father's HEART for God's FACE in the answer?

The Pilgrim

The way is dark, my Father! cloud on cloud
Is gathering o'er my head; and loud
The thunders roar above me. See, I stand
Like one bewildered; Father! take my hand,
    And through the gloom lead safely home
        Thy child.

The way is long, my Father! and my soul
Longs for the rest and quiet of the goal;
While yet I journey through this land,
Keep me from wandering. Father! take my hand,
    Quickly and straight lead to heaven's gate
        Thy child.

The path is rough, my Father! many a thorn
Has pierced me, and my weary feet are torn,
And bleeding, mark the way. Yet Thy command
Bids me press forward. Father! take my hand,
    Then, safe and blest, lead up to rest
        Thy child.

The cross is heavy, Father, Father! I have borne
So long, and still do bear it. Let my worn
And fainting spirit rise to that blessed land
Where crowns are given. Father! take my hand,
    And reaching down, lead to Thy crown
        Thy child.

The way *is* dark, my child! but leads to light:
I would not have thee always walk by sight.
My dealings, now, thou canst not understand;
I meant it so; but I will take thy hand,
    And through the gloom lead safely home
        My child.

The way *is* long, my child! but it shall be
Not one step longer than is good for thee;
And thou shalt know, at last, when thou shalt stand
Close to the gate, how I did take thy hand,
    And, quick and straight, lead to heaven's gate
        My child.

The path *is* rough, my child! but oh! how sweet
Will be the rest, for weary pilgrims meet,
When thou shalt reach the border of that land
To which I lead thee, as I take thy hand,
    And, safe and blest, with Me shall rest
        My child.

The cross *is* heavy, child! yet there is One
Who bore a heavier for thee: My Son,
My well-beloved; with *Him* bear thine, and stand
With *Him*, at last; and from thy Father's hand,
    Thy cross laid down, receive thy crown,
        My child.

"My cup runneth over"

— Psalm 23:5 —

THERE is a process needed in all our souls, that we should be able to say: "My cup runneth over." This is not the experience of the first part of the Psalm. There, in being able to say: "The Lord is my Shepherd," it is easy to add: "I shall not **want**." Accordingly, we find the Shepherd's care expressed in the green pastures and still waters of His providing, that the soul thus **invigorated** (for this is the meaning of "restore," as food or rest restores) may walk "in the paths of righteousness for His Name's sake." But in the latter part of the Psalm there is a marked change. The green pastures and waters of rest are no longer present to the soul, but the valley of the **shadow of death**. This is commonly taken to mean a death-bed. Practically the experience of this Psalm is often only reached on a death-bed. But it ought not to be so; and that this is not the thought of the passage may be clear from the words: "Surely goodness and mercy shall follow me **all the days of my life**."

There is a greater death than ours to hearts that know the Lord. Surely it is the shadow of **His** death, the death of Psalm 22, that lies upon the whole scene of this world. The world in which our Lord was crucified is the valley of the shadow of death. Oh! for hearts to be more affected by His death. How far has the whole scene here closed for us, enwrapped in the shadow of that greatest death of all?

What is there then left for us? **"THOU art with me."** It is **the Shepherd Himself** proved more to the heart than all His precious care. **He** is more than all He can give. When the soul reaches this in its growth, shut up to Himself in a world closed to it by His cross, it is not merely that "I shall not want," but "My Cup **runneth over**." He has brought us into the reality and blessedness of His own experience! He Himself, who once as Man on earth could say: "The Lord is the portion of My cup," now fills that cup to overflowing for us.

Look Up!

One upward look, my God, to Thee,
    When weary of the strife;
When tempted, downcast, sore to be
    About the straits of life;
One upward look, I turn to Thee,
    And peace steals o'er my soul,
Calm reigns, as Thy blest face I see,
    My care on Thee I roll.

A calm that's understood by none
    Save those who know Thy love;
It fills with rest the heart of one
    Who sees Thee there above,
Upon the throne of grace, so free
    To all who would draw near
To find their sorrow met by Thee—
    Thy love that casts out fear.

Lord, I would ever be so nigh
    That I might quickly see
The blessed guidance of Thine eye,
    That look that's turned on me:
It may be one of sympathy,
    Or tender, loving care;
For all that now distresses me
    Is known by Thee up there.

I joy to meet that look of love,
    It cheers my fainting soul,
It lifts me up the storm above,
    It draws me towards the goal.
To me Thou dost Thy strength impart
    To tread the desert road,
With lighter steps and thankful heart
    For all the grace of God.

Psalm 23

"The Lord is my Shepherd; I shall not want."

I shall not want **REST**.
> *"He maketh me to lie down in green pastures."*

I shall not want **REFRESHMENT**.
> *"He leadeth me beside the still waters."*

I shall not want **REVIVING**.
> *"He restoreth* my soul."*

I shall not want **GUIDANCE**.
> *"He leadeth me in the paths of righteousness for His name's sake."*

I shall not want **COMPANIONSHIP**.
> *"Yea, though I walk through the valley of the shadow of death, I will fear no evil: for Thou art with me."*

I shall not want **COMFORT**.
> *"Thy rod and Thy staff they comfort me."*

I shall not want **SUSTENANCE**.
> *"Thou preparest a table before me in the presence of mine enemies."*

I shall not want **JOY**.
> *"Thou anointest my head with oil."*

I shall not want **ANYTHING**.
> *"My cup runneth over."*

I shall not want **ANYTHING IN THIS LIFE**.
> *"Surely goodness and mercy shall follow me all the days of my life."*

I shall not want **ANYTHING IN ETERNITY**.
> *"And I will dwell in the house of the Lord for ever."*

*J N Darby New Translation – Reviveth.

"Ah, Lord God! behold, I cannot ..."
Jeremiah 1:6

* * * *

"Is there anything too hard for Me?"
Jeremiah 32:27

* * * *

"Now shalt thou see what I will do."
Exodus 6:1

* * * *

"Fear thou not; for I am with thee: be not dismayed; for I am thy God: I will strengthen thee; yea, I will help thee; yea, I will uphold thee with the right hand of My righteousness."
Isaiah 41:10

In Time of Trouble...

SAY—

> FIRST: He brought me here; it is by His will I am in this strait place; in that I will rest.
>
> NEXT: He will here keep me in His love, and give me grace in this trial to behave as His child.
>
> THEN: He will make the trial a blessing—teaching me the lessons He means me to learn, and working in me the grace He intends for me.
>
> LAST: In His good time He can bring me out again—how and when, HE KNOWS.

SAY—

> I AM HERE: (1) By God's appointment.
> (2) In His keeping.
> (3) Under His training.
> (4) For His time.
>
> *(Psalm 50:15).*

OUR OWN STRENGTH IS JUST OUR WEAKNESS, AS OUR WEAKNESS REALIZED WILL BE OUR WAY TO STRENGTH—A STRENGTH NOT OUR OWN.

If you are a child of God, wherever you propose to nestle there your Heavenly Father will plant a thorn, until you are driven, like a bird, from spray to spray and from leaf to leaf, and taught by painful experience that God, and God alone, is from everlasting to everlasting the "dwelling-place" of His people.

Comfort in Sorrow
JOHN 11:6

THE truest heart that ever loved
    Could give its object pain—
Could bear to see the suffering
    That brought the untold gain.

The mightiest hand that ever moved
    Could wait to bring relief—
"Two days'" apparent heedlessness
    Of nature's deepest grief.

Would they have missed that sacred thing—
    His sympathy—His tears—
Scene on which breaking hearts have leaned
    For nineteen hundred years.

The wonder-working word that gave
    Their loved one back again,
Seems scarce so precious as the groan
    That proved He shared their pain.

O heart, that loves so perfectly!
    Thou often waitest still,
And blessed are the emptied hearts
    Thy sympathy can fill.

A Commonplace Life

A COMMONPLACE life, we say and we sigh;
But why should we sigh as we say?
The commonplace sun in the commonplace sky
Makes up the commonplace day.
The moon and the stars are commonplace things,
And the flowers that bloom, and the bird that sings.
But dark were the world and sad our lot,
If the flowers failed, and the sun shone not.
And God, who studied each separate soul,
Out of commonplace lives made His beautiful whole.

Strength in Looking Up

THERE is always strength in looking to God; but if the mind rest upon the weakness otherwise than to cast it upon God it becomes unbelief. Difficulties may come in. God may allow many things to arise to prove our weakness; but the simple path of faith is to go on, not looking beforehand at what we have to do, but reckoning upon the help that we shall need and find when the time arrives. The sense that we are nothing makes us glad to forget ourselves, and then it is that Christ becomes everything to the soul.

"He knoweth them that trust in Him"

"The Lord is good, a strong hold in the day of trouble; and He knoweth them that trust in Him." NAHUM 1:7

The Bible student may not always find the minor prophets so interesting as many other parts of the Bible. How absorbing in interest, for instance, are the four gospels, telling us as they do of the Life of lives; or the epistles, that unfold to us the wonderful scheme of Christianity—the moral triumph of God in a world of ruin; or the Pentateuch, that tells us of the first beginning of things, and prefigures, in wonderful type and shadow, that which should come to pass in the person of Jesus! "The testimony of Jesus is the spirit of prophecy."

But individual exercise is, at the root of things, essentially the same in all ages, and here and there in the minor prophets—as much, surely, a part of Scripture as the gospels or epistles—we find experience which appeals to us now as freshly as when first written.

True, we increase by the knowledge of God, and God being more fully revealed now than then, we should walk in the light of that fuller revelation. Thus many an Old Testament scripture yields peculiarly real instruction and comfort when viewed in the full light of the revelation of God. The Psalms are pre-eminently an example of this.

And the scripture before us is a very precious example among many. A little meditation on it will be profitable.

"The Lord is good"

It is one of the greatest triumphs of God that He has given the knowledge of His perfect goodness to many a frail man, so that the most untoward circumstances, the deepest bereavement or sorrow or suffering, cannot shake his confidence. Even Job said, "Though He slay me, yet will I trust in Him." But we are permitted to go a step further. We know that whatever is brought upon the believer by God is not merely the product of divine goodness, but the positive plannings of divine love. However severe the trial and deep the pain and trying the exercise, it does but the more convince us of that clear, warm love that makes no mistakes—a love which is so deeply concerned that the divine purpose should be worked out in us that it will not shrink from adopting means that may at the moment bring the tear to the eye and make the whole frame wince and quiver. "Nevertheless afterward it yieldeth the peaceable fruit of righteousness unto them which are exercised thereby" (*Hebrews 12:11*).

Ask that dying saint, racked with pain, lying, it may be, in a damp cottage with no earthly comfort; ask that bereaved one, out of whose life has passed for ever with the silence of death the object of deepest affection, and each will answer, with brightening eye and kindling voice, "*The Lord is good.*"

"A strong hold in the day of trouble"

Ay, the One we turn to in our stress, and who never fails or disappoints us; the One who never flatters us; the One who looks right down to the roots of pride and self-sufficiency; the One who sees the idol in the heart or the little foxes that spoil the tender vines; yet the One who remembers we are but dust, and who makes a way of escape for us, that we may be able, not to escape but to bear the trial, He is *a strong hold*. What security, what rest, what comfort! No wonder our hearts and minds are *garrisoned* by the peace of God when we turn to Him in our day of trouble!

"And He knoweth them that trust in Him"

He knoweth, not we know. That we know God is evidenced in measure, at least when we can say, "The Lord is good." But here it is that *He* knows us—that *He* knows the heart that trusts in Him.

Peter could lay open his heart to Him and say, "Lord, Thou knowest all things; Thou knowest that I love Thee." How sweet in trouble, when we dare not openly boast that we trust Him, that we have the confidence that He knows that we trust in Him—One who will never fail the simple trust of a dependent soul!

GOD IS BETTER THAN OUR *FAITH*

WE once said to a dear coloured woman in Jamaica, much tried in her circumstances, "God is better to us than our *fears*."

She answered with a quick smile, "Yes, and God is better to us than our *faith*."

I confess that I stood rebuked, and felt I was in the presence of one taught in the school of God. I looked on that woman as a triumph of Christianity, as a complete answer to the first question raised in the Bible, a question doubting God's goodness and love, *"Yea, hath God said?"* The object of Satan was achieved when he instilled doubt into man's heart at the fall. God's triumph over Satan is proclaimed when a weak saint is found triumphing over afflictions, praising Him for trials, rejoicing in tribulation. "Perfect love casteth out fear." To trust Him in the dark and adore Him for His ways, is indeed a vindication of God over evil.

✻ ✻ ✻

"BRINGING INTO CAPTIVITY EVERY THOUGHT"
2 Corinthians 10:5.

If I *think* of my sorrow,
I bear the impress of my sorrow.
If I *think* of the world,
I bear the impress of the world.
If I *think* of Christ,
I bear the impress of Christ.

2 Corinthians 3:18.

The Truest Comfort in Sorrow

NEARLY twenty years ago I was told by my doctor that I was suffering from a certain disease. From what I knew of that disease, I believed that I could not live more than six months. How did the doctor's information affect me? I can humbly and truthfully testify that it filled me with deepest joy. I did not want to die. I was young. Life was sweet to me. The physical process of death was not inviting. But one thought filled my heart with an ecstasy of joy, "In six months' time I shall actually see MY SAVIOUR."

God raised me up. For two years I had a strenuous fight for life. Death contested stubbornly every inch of ground on the road to recovery. During those two very grave years the knowledge that my eternal future was assured was my stay and comfort and joy.

I can conceive of nothing more terrible than to be in sorrow, especially as to one's own physical condition, without the knowledge of *a personal Saviour.*

There came a moment in my history, over forty years ago, when I learned that I was a guilty sinner before God, that I could not save myself, nor help to save myself; that if I were to be saved, God must do it. I learned that the Lord Jesus Christ had died on the cross for sinners—for me, there to atone for sins, and enable God *righteously* to forgive the repentant sinner. And,

> "*I came to Jesus as I was,*
> *Weary and worn and sad,*
> *I found in Him my resting place,*
> *And He has made me glad.*"

The following plain, simple texts helped me. May they help you. You may be saved HERE and NOW.

Let your heart go out in real trust to the Lord Jesus Christ, and salvation is yours on the spot.

> "God so loved the world, that He gave His only begotten Son, *that* WHOSOEVER *believeth* in Him should not perish, but HAVE *everlasting life*" (John 3:16).

* * * * * *

> "Verily, verily, I say unto you, He that heareth My word, and believeth on Him that sent Me, HATH *everlasting life,* and SHALL NOT COME *into condemnation*; but IS *passed from death unto life*" (John 5:24).

* * * * * *

> "To Him [Jesus] give all the prophets witness, that through His name whosoever believeth in Him shall receive remission of sins" (Acts 10:43).

* * * * * *

> "Believe on the Lord Jesus Christ, and thou shalt be saved" (Acts 16:31).

* * * * * *

> "If thou shalt confess with thy mouth the Lord Jesus, and shalt believe in thine heart that God hath raised Him from the dead, *thou shalt be* SAVED" (Romans 10:9).

Put your simple trust in the Lord Jesus Christ, and these verses out of God's unchanging Word will assure you of salvation, forgiveness, eternal life. God grant that they may.

"Behold, NOW is the accepted time; Behold, NOW is the day of salvation" (2 Corinthians 6:2).

"Not Now"

Mark 5:18-19

NOT NOW, my child—a little more rough tossing,
  A little longer on the billows' foam,
A few more journeyings in the desert-darkness,
  And THEN the sunshine of thy Father's home.

NOT NOW,—for I have wand'rers in the distance,
  And thou must call them in with patient love;
NOT NOW,—for I have sheep upon the mountains,
  And thou must follow them where'er they rove.

NOT NOW,—for I have lov'd ones sad and weary;
  Wilt thou not cheer them with a kindly smile?
Sick ones, who need thee in their lonely sorrow;
  Wilt thou not tend them yet a little while?

NOT NOW,—for wounded hearts are sorely bleeding,
  And thou must teach those widow'd hearts to sing;
NOT NOW,—for orphans' tears are thickly falling;
  They must be gathered 'neath some sheltering wing.

NOT NOW,—for many a hungry one is pining;
  Thy willing hand must be outstretched and free;
Thy Father hears the mighty cry of anguish,
  And gives His answering messages to thee.

NOT NOW,—for dungeon walls look stern and gloomy,
  And pris'ners' sighs sound strangely on the breeze—
MAN'S pris'ners, but thy Saviour's noble free-men;
  Hast thou no ministry of love for these?

NOT NOW,—for hell's eternal gulf is yawning,
  And souls are perishing in hopeless sin,—
Jerusalem's bright gates are standing open—
  Go to the banished ones, and fetch them in!

Go with the Name of Jesus to the dying,
  And speak that Name in all its living power;
Why should thy fainting heart grow chill and weary?
  Canst thou not WATCH WITH ME one little hour?

One little hour! and THEN the glorious crowning,
　　The golden harp-strings and the victor's palm,—
One little hour!—and THEN the Hallelujah!
　　Eternity's long, deep thanksgiving Psalm.

"Jesus Christ the SAME yesterday, and to-day, and for ever"

"**ABLE** *to succour*
　　them that are tempted."
　　　　　　　　　　(HEBREWS 2:18).

"**ABLE** *also to save*
　　them to the uttermost."
　　　　　　　　　　(HEBREWS 7:25).

"**ABLE** *to make*
　　all grace abound toward you."
　　　　　　　　　　(2 CORINTHIANS 9:8).

"**ABLE** *to do*
　　exceeding abundantly above all
　　that we ask or think."
　　　　　　　　　　(EPHESIANS 3:20).

"**ABLE** *to keep*
　　you from falling, and to present
　　you faultless."
　　　　　　　　　　(JUDE 24).

The Peacock's Feathers

"Gavest thou the goodly wings unto the peacocks?"
(*Job 39:13*)

WHO is there that has not gazed with wonder and admiration at those "goodly wings" with their ever-varying tints, their rich and glorious effects of colour and brilliant metallic lustre?

Of all the beauteous feathered tribe the peacock is perhaps the most gorgeously arrayed, and we can but admire the beauty of design in the plumage of this creature of God.

But is this pleasure to our eyes, think you, the object to which our attention is drawn in the words before us? I think the One who speaks here would have us consider something deeper.

It was at a time when I was in much weakness and suffering, I was regarding the beauty of some peacock's feathers on my mantelpiece, and the thoughts that came were a comfort to me, and perhaps may be so to some others in affliction.

I considered how all the different particles of colouring matter had travelled from the root of each feather up the long stem, and into the tiny multitudinous fibres of which the feather is composed, and were deposited in those fibres with such marvellous accuracy; each tint, each shade just in its right proportion, and in its right place. How wonderful that in the journey from root to tip the different pigments do not get mingled, nor yet unduly separated! If either colour were out of proportion either in quantity or position, even by a few grains, the harmony of the whole would be marred.

But no! not a shade out of place. Each infinitesimal particle fits itself in beautiful order into its appointed fibre with the most minute exactness, and the result is the grand and bright design which we so admire.

Thus, surely, the same Hand that has so magnificently clothed a mere bird, is at work in the daily details of the surroundings of "His own." It is "God that performeth *all* things for me," and if He manifests such minute exactness in order that the beauty of His handiwork be seen in a bird's feathers, He surely is taking *no less* care for me. And if not a fibre is permitted to get too much or too little of the blue, the purple, or the gold, so is measured to me each day, each hour, each moment, I may say each varied circumstance, even the most trivial that goes to make up my life.

Oh! what a comfort it is to know that *such* a Hand is, with unerring skill, shaping my pathway, measuring each detail of things left out and things brought in; all blending in wisely measured proportion towards the formation of His bright design. Here, then, let me rest, confident that He who allows no confusion to mar "the goodly wings" of the peacock, will allow nothing untoward to intrude or to mar what He is performing for me. "As for God, His way is *perfect*," and not only so, but "He maketh *my* way perfect."

On another occasion the lovely colours themselves seemed to speak to me. There is the bright green which appears to express freshness, gladness, perhaps praise, the outcome of gladness. We have our happy days, when our hearts sing unto Him who has put a new song into our mouth.

Next the violet in the heart of the pattern always makes me think of that lowly submission to chastening which brings our hearts so closely into touch with His holy love, and makes our suffering days so to partake of heavenly grace.

Blue is the heavenly colour, and in one light will be seen helping to form both the violet and the green.

Then the more sombre brown may perhaps tell us of the ordinary homely days when earthly things seem to predominate, and we see but little that we think of any worth. This is a sort of background for the more vivid tints. Only take it to the light and it will shine with lustrous gold, reminding us of the words of Scripture that "surely goodness and mercy shall follow me *all the days* of my life."

But what of those many ribs all along the stalk of each feather, which do not appear to have any part in the beautiful pattern traced out at the tip? May they not remind us of the earlier days of our life before our conversion, when we knew nothing of the work of God in us? Yet when seen in the sunshine, they, too, will be found to have a golden brightness—"lustred with His love," even when we knew it not. And thus, if looked at in the light of Scripture, where God's precious things are made known, we can discern the halo of His *loving* kindness and *tender* mercy over "all the days of our life."

A faithful God, "wonderful in counsel, and excellent in working," is He with whom we have to do. And why, we may ask, is He taking all this infinite care for us? Ah! He has a bright design indeed. He has purposed that we should be for the glory of His beloved Son. We are dear to Him as belonging to that dear Son, and in the soon-coming day something of His glorious image will be seen to have been wrought in us. "When He hath tried me, I shall come forth as gold." "Changed into the same image from glory to glory." "I shall be satisfied, when I awake, with Thy likeness."

ॐ ॐ ॐ

And is it so! I shall be like Thy Son,
Is this the grace which He for me has won?
Father of glory, thought beyond all thought,
In glory, to His own blest likeness brought.

Nor I alone, Thy loved ones all, complete
In glory round Thee there with joy shall meet,
All like Thee, for Thy glory like Thee, Lord,
Object supreme of all, by all adored.

Perfect through Suffering

IS this the way, my Father? — 'Tis, my child;
Thou must pass through the tangled, dreary wild,
If thou would'st reach the city undefiled—
      Thy peaceful home above.

❋   ❋   ❋

My Father, it is dark! — Child, take my hand;
Cling close to Me, I'll lead thee through the land;
Trust My all-seeing care, so shalt thou stand
      'Midst glory bright above.

❋   ❋   ❋

My footsteps seem to slide! — Child, only raise
Thine eyes to Me, then in these slippery ways
I'll hold thy goings up, and thou shalt praise
      Me for each step above.

❋   ❋   ❋

Father, I am weary! — Child, lean thy head
Upon My breast; it was My love that spread
Thy rugged path; hope on, till I have said,
      "Rest, rest for aye, above."

Peerless Worth

*"What have I to do any more with idols?
I have heard Him, and observed Him."*

HOSEA 14:8

HAST thou seen Him, heard Him, known Him?
    Is not thine a captured heart?
"Chief among ten thousand" own Him,
    Joyful choose the better part.

Idols, once they won thee, charmed thee,
    Lovely things of time and sense;
Gilded, thus does sin disarm thee,
    Honey'd, lest they turn thee hence.

What has stript the seeming beauty
    From the idols of the earth?
Not the sight of right or duty,
    But the sight of peerless worth.

Not the crushing of those idols,
    With its bitter void and smart,
But the beaming of His beauty,
    The unveiling of His heart.

Who extinguishes their taper,
    Till they hail the rising sun?
Who discards the robe of winter,
    Till the summer has begun?

'Tis that look that melted Peter,
    'Tis that face that Stephen saw,
'Tis that heart that wept with Mary
    Can alone from idols draw.

Draw—and win, and fill completely,
    Till the cup o'erflow the brim,
What have we to do with idols
    Who have companied with Him?

Counting on God for everything

WE can count on Him for everything. He is good; nothing good will He withhold from those who walk before Him. The soul closes in the conscious feeling—"Blessed is the man that trusteth in Thee." And how true it is! Nothing can disturb, nothing is beyond His power—nothing of which His love cannot take charge for us—nothing which His wisdom does not know how to deal with for blessing. And the heart knows His love to count on it, and that blessed is the man that puts his trust in Him.

Paul Gerhardt... ..alone with God

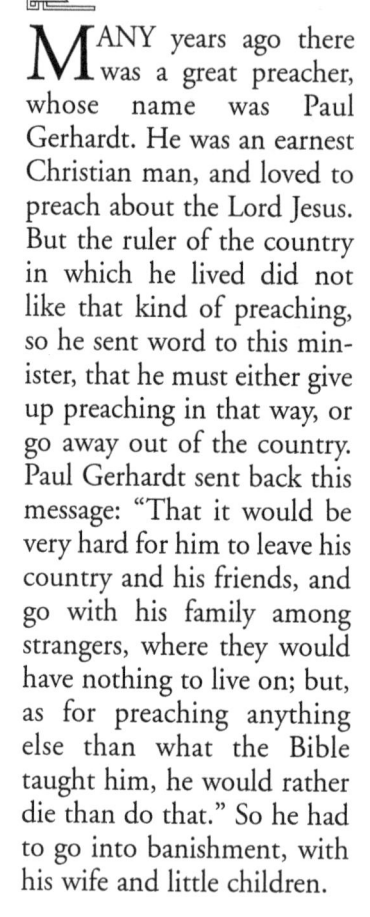

MANY years ago there was a great preacher, whose name was Paul Gerhardt. He was an earnest Christian man, and loved to preach about the Lord Jesus. But the ruler of the country in which he lived did not like that kind of preaching, so he sent word to this minister, that he must either give up preaching in that way, or go away out of the country. Paul Gerhardt sent back this message: "That it would be very hard for him to leave his country and his friends, and go with his family among strangers, where they would have nothing to live on; but, as for preaching anything else than what the Bible taught him, he would rather die than do that." So he had to go into banishment, with his wife and little children.

At the end of their first day's journey they came into a wood and rested for the night at a little inn they found there. The little children were crying with hunger, and clinging to their mother; but she had no food to give, and no money to buy any with. She had tried to keep up all day, but now she began to cry too. This made Paul Gerhardt have a very heavy heart. He left his family, and went alone into the dark wood to pray. It was a time of great trouble to him, and there was no one to whom he could go for help but to God.

While he was alone in the wood praying, a text of Scripture came into his mind. It seemed to him as if an angel had come and whispered it to him:

"COMMIT THY WAY UNTO THE LORD; TRUST ALSO IN HIM; AND HE SHALL BRING IT TO PASS." *(Psalm 37:5).*

This gave him great comfort. "Yes," he said to himself, "though I am banished from my home and friends, and do not know where to take my wife and children for a shelter, yet God, MY God, sees me in this dark wood. He knows all about us. Now is the time to trust in Him. He will show me through; He will 'bring it to pass.'"

He was so happy in thinking on this text, and so thankful to God for bringing it into his mind, that he walked up and down under the trees, and made some verses on it, which were afterwards written down and printed. Each verse begins with two or three words of the text, so that, when you have read through the hymn, you get the whole text. Perhaps you would like to read the verses before we finish the story.

Here they are:—

Commit thy way, O weeper—
   The cares that fret thy soul—
To thine Almighty Keeper,
   Who makes the world to roll.

Unto the Lord, who quieteth
   The wind, and cloud, and sea;
Oh! doubt not He provideth
   A footpath, too, for thee.

Trust also, for 'tis useless
   To murmur and forbode;
The Almighty arm is doubtless
   Full strong to bear thy load.

In Him hide all thy sorrow
   And bid thy fears good night;
He'll make a glorious morrow
   To crown thy head with light.

And He shall bring it near thee,
   The good thou long hast sought;
Though now it seems to fly thee,
   Thou shalt, ere long, be brought

To pass from grief to gladness,
   From night to clearest day;
When doubts, and fears, and sadness
   Shall all have passed away.

When he had finished making these verses he went into the house. He told his wife about the sweet text that had come into his mind, and repeated to her the verses he had made upon it. She soon dried up her tears, and began to be as cheerful and trustful as her husband was. The children were in bed and asleep. The husband and wife knelt down together and prayed, and resolved to "commit their way unto the Lord," and leave it for Him to "bring to pass" as He saw fit. Then, after writing down his sweet verses, they went to bed.

Before they had fallen asleep a great noise was heard at the door of the inn. It seemed as though some important person was knocking there. When the landlord opened the door, a man on horseback was standing before it. He said, in a loud voice—

"I am a messenger. I come from Duke Christian, and I am trying to find a minister named Paul Gerhardt, who has just been banished. Do you know whether he has passed this way?"

"Paul Gerhardt?" said the landlord; "why, yes, he is in this house; but he has just gone to bed. I can't disturb him now."

"But you must," said the messenger. "I have a very important letter for him from the Duke; let me see him at once." So the landlord went upstairs and told Gerhardt, who came down to see what all this could be about.

The messenger handed him a large, sealed letter; and, to his great joy, he read in it that the good Duke Christian had heard of the intended banishment of himself and family, and had written to him saying, "Come into my country, Paul Gerhardt, and you shall have a house, and home, and plenty to live on, and liberty to preach the Gospel just as much as you please."

Then he went up and told his wife, and they praised God for His love; and the next morning they started off with glad hearts and cheerful feet to their new home.

❋ ❋ ❋

I Know Not!

I KNOW not what of trial or of joy
   May lie before me in the untrod way;
But yet I know sufficient grace is mine
   For each succeeding day.

I know not whether there may partings be,
   The rending of earth's ties that are so sweet;
But this I know, that rest for breaking hearts
   Is found at Jesu's feet.

I know not whether I shall serve Him where
   The praise of man sheds glamour over toil,
Or in the lonely field of faith and prayer
   Wait for the share of spoil.

I know not—yet I know that He plans all,
   All that God chooseth is for ever best,
And this He gives to those who only seek,
   His will, and in Him rest.

"Thy faithfulness reacheth unto the clouds"
(Psalm 36:5)

The inner side of every cloud
    Is bright and shining.
Then let us turn our clouds about,
And always wear them inside out,
    To show the lining.

Lean and Pray

WHEN you run the Christian race,
    And are footsore,
You would find the hills less steep,
And the little ruts less deep,
    If you leaned more.

When you're weary of the fight,
    And are heartsore,
You would find your foes less strong,
And the fight would seem less long,
    If you prayed more.

"Thou hast made me exceeding glad with Thy countenance."

NOT with one lingering thought of disappointment,
   But with a glad, and an untroubled rest;
Not with a stifled sigh, or hidden tear-drop,
   Trying to think that all is for the best.

Not an attempt at mournful resignation,
   Sadly regretting all that might have been,
Fearing to follow such a darksome pathway,
   Where all is so mysterious and unseen.

No! but with gladdened eyes now upward turning
   Unto the glory of the Saviour's face,
Which gazes down on me with love unfathomed,—
   'Tis thus alone I learn to know His peace.

Whilst I am gazing at that radiant glory,
   The doubts and fears, and tremblings all must flee,
Naught can I see now but the face of Jesus,—
   The Son of God, who gave Himself for me!

He "gave *Himself*"—oh! mystery, oh! wonder,
   How great that gift I ne'er can fully know;
For me He gave Himself in His perfection,
   The wrath of God for me to undergo.

And now He whispers, "'Tis *thyself* I ask for,
   Leave Me to choose which way I lead thee home.
The path can only shine and still grow brighter,
   Until the perfect day be fully come."

Stray Thoughts

Anything *with* Thy smile.
Anything *but* Thy frown.

Blessed be His name, it is part of His covenant to visit us with the rod, little as we may be worthy of it.

Did I not think my Teacher as faithful as He is infallible, there is no book I should so fear to handle as the book of God.

The hottest of all furnaces in which He tries faith is that heated with our own sins.

There is something sweet in being pruned by a wounded hand.

Have you ever marked His steps, His gentleness, when bringing a painful message?

It is almost worth having a wound to prove how tenderly He heals.

Oh! what sweet truths He often whispers to His saints from behind clouds.

❁ MANNA BY THE WAY ❁

The parings and crumbs of glory that fall under His (Christ's) table in heaven, a shower like a thin May-mist of His love, would make me green, and sappy, and joyful till the summer sun of an eternal glory break up.

I urge upon you a **nearer** communion with Christ, and a **growing** communion. There are curtains to be drawn by, in Christ, that one never saw, and new foldings of love in Him.

I wonder what He meaneth to put such a slave at the board-head, at His own elbow; but I dare not refuse to be loved; the cause is not in me why He hath looked upon me, and loved me, for He got nothing of me; it is good, cheap love.

Put Christ's love to the trial, and put upon it burdens, and then it will appear love indeed. We employ not His love; and, therefore, we know it not. I verily count more of the sufferings of my Lord than of this world's lustred and over-gilded glory.

Now, for myself, know I am fully agreed with my Lord. Christ hath put the Father and me in other's arms, many a sweet bargain He made before, and He hath made this among the rest, I reign as King over my crosses.

The dross of my trials gathered a scum of fears in the fire, doubtings, impatience, unbelief, challenging of Providence as sleeping, and not regarding my sorrow; but my goldsmith, Christ, was pleased to take off the scum, and burn it in the fire.

Faith is the better for the free air and the sharp winter-storm in its face. Grace withereth without adversity.

You may yourself ebb and flow, rise and fall, wax and wane; but your Lord is this day as He was yesterday; and it is your comfort that your salvation is not rolled upon wheels of your own making; neither have you to do with a Christ of your own shaping. I see the Lord making use of this fire to scour His vessels from their rust. Oh! that my will were silent, and as "a child weaned from the breasts." *(Psalm 131.)*

❁ ❁ ❁ ❁

— "BE STILL!" —

"Rest in the Lord, and wait patiently for Him."
[*Literally*—"Be silent to God, and let Him mould thee."—LUTHER.]

FROM vintages of sorrow are deepest joys distilled,
And the cup outstretched for healing is oft at Marah filled;
God leads to joy thro' weeping, to quietness thro' strife;
Through yielding unto conquest, through death to endless life.
Be still! He hath enrolled thee for the Kingdom and the Crown.
Be silent! Let Him mould thee, who calleth thee His own.

"What will it be?"

(1 CORINTHIANS 2:9-10)

WHAT will it be when all the toil is ended?
    When we have conquered in the last fierce strife?
When the bright portals of our home are entered?
    Pilgrims no longer—heirs of endless life!
Gone the last dust our weary feet have gather'd—
    Wiped the last drop from off the aching brow;
Safe in the presence of our God and Father,
    Whose strength supports us in the desert now.

What will it be when the effulgent glory
    Of day eternal it is ours to see?
When (for the first time in our life's short story)
    Pure from all trace of sin our ways shall be.
When, of God's household, in that land elysian,
    Where not a thought can mar our perfect rest,
Where not a cloud shall dim the spirit's vision;
    Joint-heirs with Christ, we shall be fully blest.

What will it be to see the hidden meaning
    Of every trial we have met below?
To trace the secret of our Father's training,
    Where faith gained spoils from many a vanquished foe?
All that seems dark to our imperfect vision,
    The light of heaven at once will render plain;
Deeper our joy through that all-wise provision—
    Suffering awhile, ere with our Lord we reign.

What will it be? Oh, what no thought hath measured,
    No eye hath seen, no ear of man hath heard!
Unsearchable the riches Christ hath treasur'd,
    Yet all is sure to him who trusts His Word!
On then! though rough and dark the path and dreary;
    All toil and pain the end will well repay!
Onward and upward! we may now be weary;
    With Jesus soon, to share His home for aye!

The Tapestry Weavers

Let us take to our hearts a lesson—no lesson can braver be—
From the ways of the tapestry weavers on the other side of the sea.
Above their heads the pattern hangs, they study it with care;
The while their fingers deftly work, their eyes are fastened there.
They tell this curious thing, besides, of the patient, plodding weaver—
He works on the wrong side evermore, but works for the right side ever:
It is only when the weaving stops, and the web is loosed and turned
That he sees his real handiwork, that his marvellous skill is learned.
Ah! the sight of its delicate beauty, how it pays him for all his cost!
No rarer, daintier work than this was ever done by the frost.
Then the master bringeth him golden hire, and giveth him praise as well,
And how happy the heart of the weaver is no tongue but his own can tell.

❀   ❀   ❀   ❀   ❀   ❀   ❀

The years of man are the looms of God, let down from the place of the sun,
Wherein we are weaving alway, till the wondrous web is done—
Weaving slowly, but weaving surely, a robe of spotless white,
We may not see how the right side looks, but can only weave in the light:
But looking above for the pattern, no weaver need have fear;
Only let him look clear into heaven, the Perfect Pattern is there:
If he keeps the face of our Saviour for ever and always in sight,
His toil shall be sweeter than honey, his weaving is sure to be right.
And when his task is ended, and the web is turned and shown,
He shall hear the voice of The Master—it shall say to him, "Well done";
For the Lord shall descend from heaven, to bear all His loved ones home,
And then for his wage shall give him, not COIN, but a GOLDEN CROWN.

Stripped but Blessed

"PERFECT and upright, and one that feared God, and eschewed evil." Such was Job's character, given by God—no mean one, especially as it was earned in what we believe were pre-Abrahamic days, with no general light of revelation.

He was blessed, too, as godliness was in those days, with abundance of this world's goods. "And there were born unto him seven sons and three daughters. His substance also was seven thousand sheep, and three thousand camels, and five hundred yoke of oxen, and five hundred she asses, and a very great household; so that this man was the greatest of all the men of the east."

All was outwardly prosperous, but God chose the *best* man on the earth (see Job 1:8) to be blessed by discovering Himself to Job, and discovering, necessarily, Job to himself. The steps to this end are intensely interesting.

God asks Satan, "Hast thou considered My servant Job, that there is none like him in the earth?" Satan, in reply, says in effect, "Strip him, and he will curse Thee to Thy face." Satan sought his fall, God sought his blessing; Satan wished him to curse God, God desired that he should abhor himself.

Satan gets leave from God to strip Job. With malignant energy he sets to work, and in one day he brings the greatest man in all the east into abject poverty and visits him with sore bereavement.

Blow after blow falls upon Job of such a crushing nature and in such rapidity that one marvels at the comment of the Holy Ghost on his conduct in it all: "In all this did not Job sin with his lips." What self-restraint! What a triumph for God so far! What a defeat for Satan, who predicted the deep and bitter curse if God touched his possessions! The tongue is an unruly member. Says James, "If any man offend not in word, the same is a perfect man, and able also to bridle the whole body." And Job, up to this point, behaved perfectly.

Scripture gives us in detail how Satan sought to effect his purpose.

A messenger comes with the serious news that the Sabeans had robbed him of his oxen and asses, and but one servant had escaped to tell the tale. Heavy as the blow was, it only meant that part of his property was gone; but lo! another messenger arrives to say that fire from heaven had burnt up his sheep, and yet another tells him that the Chaldeans, in three bands, had captured his camels.

Poor Job! By no fault of his own, by no carelessness of his, in one moment, fortune, wealth, position are swept away. He is absolutely penniless. Still, wife and children are left him.

But lo! a more crushing blow, heavier than all the rest. A great wind from the wilderness had smitten the four corners of the house in which his sons and daughters were feasting, and had killed them all.

Agonising as it is for a man to be suddenly stripped and become absolutely poor, it is nothing to the anguish of parting for ever from some loved one. At a later date David in anguish wailed, as he heard of the death of Bathsheba's child, "I shall go to him, but he shall not return to me." And years after the same father lamented with profound pathos over his rebellious but dead son, "O my son Absalom, my son, my son Absalom! would God I had died for thee, O Absalom, my son, my son!"

But Job! What shall we say of him? Not one sore bereavement, but ten—all merged into one mighty, overwhelming blow! Not one child, but all! Firstborn and youngest, son and daughter, all gone at one fell swoop!

Still, he has health, inestimable boon! But lo! the malignant fiendishness of Satan would touch even that, so eager was he for Job's fall. He hisses into God's ear, "Skin for skin, yea, all that a man hath will he give for his life. But put forth Thine hand now, and touch his bone and his flesh, and he will curse Thee to Thy face." So God, who worked for Job's good, uses Satan's malignity, and gives him power to touch Job's body. Job is smitten with sore boils. In despair, he sits down among the ashes, and scrapes himself with a potsherd.

Satan listens for a loud, deep curse from Job's lips. As a last resource, he stirs up his wife to give evil advice, "Curse God, and die." But no. Job is master of his tongue, and Satan is baffled. Wonderful triumph for God! Stripped of property, bereaved of family, bereft of health, what more could Satan do? But God sees deeper, and will make Job abhor himself rather than curse God, as Satan tries to bring about.

Then Job's three friends come to comfort him; but they saw his grief was so great that none broke silence for seven days and nights. Oh! the intolerable gloom that fell on Job's spirit—and well it might.

At last Job opened his mouth, and cursed his day.* Then, through twenty-nine chapters of the book, his three friends argue from his trials that he is not righteous, but Job vehemently asserts his righteousness more and more. He says in conclusion, if it be otherwise, "Let thistles grow instead of wheat, and cockle instead of barley. The words of Job are ended."

The mouths of the three men are closed—all has been idle talk. Then Elihu's wrath is kindled against Job because he justified himself rather than God, and against his three friends, because, whilst

---

* Mark, he did not curse God—Satan's aim.

they had condemned Job, they had found no answer wherewith to convince him. He boldly charges Job with his unrighteousness, until the Lord takes up the theme, and speaks to Job out of the whirlwind.

In five short verses Job makes answer to God—a contrast to his previous speeches. The crux of the whole lies in this, "I have heard of Thee by the hearing of the ear: *but now mine eye seeth Thee.* Wherefore I abhor myself, and repent in dust and ashes." Personal dealing with God makes him a little man in his own eyes, even to the abhorrence of himself.

It was just this personal dealing with God that made Saul of Tarsus, with all his religiousness and zeal, speak of himself as chief of sinners; that made Isaiah confess that he was undone; that counsels the most upright and moral to acknowledge that even his "righteousnesses are as filthy rags."

This is the only road to true greatness, for when Job had arrived at this point God gave him a *double* portion, so that his latter end was more blessed than his beginning. Thus it ever is. Whether we are stripped of human righteousness as sinners, or stripped of self-complacency as saints, the end is always for blessing, and the truly great before God are the truly small in their own eyes.

It is all beautifully summed up by James when he says, "Behold, we count them happy which endure. Ye have heard of the patience of Job, and have seen the end of the Lord; that the Lord is pitiful, and of tender mercy."

Those who are enduring the stripping process, let them be encouraged by this prospect of pure blessing—"THE END OF THE LORD." "He is very pitiful, and of tender mercy." If exercised, Satan will not gain the advantage; God will gain the glory and we shall gain the blessing.

The Way Home

I TREAD a path—a toilsome path,
    A desert long and weary;
But yet my feet, as I press on,
    Swell not, nor e'er grow weary.

And if you ask me why is this,
    I answer, He who leads me,
My strength renews from day to day,
    With heavenly Manna feeds me.

Along the thirsty desert way
    A stream of water floweth—
A stream of heaven's refreshment sweet,
    Which His own hand bestoweth.

While, as I journey ever on,
    His power is all around me,
His strong right arm I lean upon,
    His love and grace surround me.

And on my very smallest need,
    His love is always waiting,
With deepest, truest tenderness
    That knoweth no abating.

O blessed pathway! e'en as blest
    The end that lies before me;
For heaven's light streams o'er the path,
    And lures me on to glory.

'Tis thus He ever leads me on
    Through path of toil and sorrow;
His love to-day's my happiness,
    His face my bright to-morrow.

"The Father's Care"

"Your Father knoweth"
(LUKE 12:30)
"The Father Himself loveth you"
(JOHN 16:27)
"He careth for you"
(1 PETER 5:7)

He knows, He loves, He cares,
Nothing this truth can dim,
He does the very best for those,
Who leave the choice with Him.

Oil and Wine

THERE is a balm for every pain,
    A medicine for all sorrow;
The eye turned backward to the Cross
    And forward to the morrow—
The morrow of the glory and the psalm,
    When He shall come;
The morrow of the harping and the palm,
    The welcome home.
Meantime in His beloved hands our ways,
    And on His heart the wandering heart's at rest;
And comfort for the weary one who lays
    His head upon His breast.

"Abba, Father"

* * * *

"TAKE Thy own way with me, blest Lord," I said,
    Kneeling at midnight at my bed,
And then upon my heart there fell deep dread.

What if He takes me at my word, and lead
Into the wilderness, from verdant mead
And pastures green in which His flocks do feed?

What if His way winds o'er the desert sands,
A road of pain and loss, through sun-scorched lands,
Where not a palm with grateful shadow stands?

A whisper came: "Not loss; there may be pain,
But all His dealings must be to their gain—
Who are His own"—my trust surged back again—

"To shaded Elim He doth lead." Once more
Peace swept upon my soul, as on the shore
A noiseless summer tide. The dread passed o'er.

I spake the words again, and faith said: "Yes,
The Father's loving hand can only bless—
God for His own has nought but tenderness."

"The Garment of Praise for the Spirit of Heaviness"

"BE careful for nothing; but in everything by prayer and supplication with thanksgiving, let your requests be made known unto God. And the peace of God, which passeth all understanding, shall keep your hearts and minds through Christ Jesus." *(Philippians 4:6-7).*

The peace of God instead of earthly care! What a blessed substitute! How infinite God's peace! How innumerable our cares! And yet the heart and mind that is burdened by care may find perfect relief in the enjoyment of the peace of God.

Now, what is the secret? How can this relief—and far more than relief—be found? To inure oneself to pain, as the Stoics of old, and to simulate indifference to it, is far short of the peace of God. Anyone can understand the effort of the philosopher, who sets his teeth and bravely determines to master the ills of life; but to become possessed, to be kept, or guarded, or garrisoned as a fortress held by power unconquerable, of the peace of God amid sorrows and tears and difficulties, is altogether beyond comprehension. It is none the less true.

Let us examine our passage:

"Be careful for nothing!" The word "nothing" covers the whole range of wilderness anxieties without omitting one. It does not include sin, far from it, for the simple reason that sin is in no wise contemplated in this epistle. It is not proper to the experience of the Christian, though, alas! every true believer realises its presence, and needs to be on constant guard against its subtle workings. Sin is abnormal to Christian experience—not impossible, but not normal. It is confessed and judged just on that very account.

The child of God should be most careful about sin, but apart from that he should be careful about nothing—no thing!

∾ ∾ ∾

"But in everything," here is the blessed remedy: **"by prayer and supplication with thanksgiving, let your requests be made known unto God."**

This is exercise, deep, earnest and precious. It is not carelessness nor indifference. There is prayer; there is supplication; there is making requests known to God; and there is the blending of thanksgiving with every prayer. This signifies close personal dealing with God.

"In everything," no matter how small, nor how great or complex, let each request of the burdened heart be laid before Him.

The Bible teems with instances of prayerful men, who spread all kinds of requests before God, from kings on their thrones to prisoners in chains, and never was a deaf ear turned to the lowly and believing suppliant.

Supplication is prayer intensified; it is importunity; its root idea is the sense of want; it is illustrated in the Prodigal Son. The word is oft-times used by the Apostle Paul; but it must carry no legal, or cringing, or selfish element; it must be sustained by thanksgiving; for remember that the Christian has received infinitely more than he can ever request. His blessings far exceed his greatest wants. God loves a thankful suppliant, and in this happy spirit the requests are made known to One who assuredly knows all about them, but who waits for the cries of the wearied child, so that

He may pour in the flood of His own incomprehensible peace. As God's peace enters care departs; the soul is tranquilized. No direct answer may have been gathered—the thorn may remain in the flesh—but the heart and mind are garrisoned by the deep, eternal calm that marks the throne on high. See the reflection of that calm as it shone in the face of Stephen; see it in the words of Paul: "**I am ready to be offered**"; recall it in the bold language of the three men who had to face the fiery furnace of Nebuchadnezzar, when they said: "**We are not careful to answer thee in this matter ... We will not serve thy gods, nor worship the golden image which thou hast set up.**" And witness the Son of God as their companion in that fiery ordeal.

Ay, and thousands of others of lesser fame rise to bear brilliant testimony in lives of labour for Christ or on beds of pain; in scenes of tumult or amid the bitter worries of daily desert life to the reality of that wonderful peace of God, which, weak and failing as they have been, has garrisoned heart and mind for days and months and years of varied pilgrim experiences.

༄ ༄ ༄

This is perhaps one of the very finest and most exquisite visible proofs of the genuineness of the faith of Christ. May reader and writer know the depths of God's peace better, and may that wonderful peace, as the result of prayer and supplication with thanksgiving, bring conscious relief to the heart, and brightness to the spirit, so that our step may be quickened and our very face made to reflect a little more of the glory of that place where alone the peace of God can be found.

༄ ༄ ༄

57

In the Plains of Jordan *

WE thank Thee, Lord, for weary days,
    When desert streams were dry;
And first we knew what depth of need,
    Thy love could satisfy.

Days when beneath the desert sun
    Along the toilsome road,
O'er roughest ways we walked with One—
    That One the Son of God.

We thank Thee for that rest in Him
    The weary only know;
The perfect, wondrous sympathy
    We needs must learn below.

The sweet companionship of One
    Who once the desert trod;
The glorious fellowship with One
    Upon the throne of God.

The joy no desolations here
    Can reach, or cloud, or dim;
The present Lord, the living God,
    And we alone with Him.

We know Him as we could not know
    Through heaven's golden years;
We there shall see His glorious face;
    But Mary saw His tears.

---

* This poem is variously entitled *A Word to the Weary*, *Companionship (John 11:35)*, and *The Desert Way* in other collections.

The touch that heals the broken heart
    Is never felt above;
His angels know His blessedness,
    His way-worn saints His love.

When in the glory and the rest
    We joyfully adore,
Remembering the desert way,
    We yet shall praise Him more.

Remembering how, amidst our toil,
    Our conflict and our sin,
He brought the water for our thirst,
    It cost His blood to win.

And now in perfect peace we go,
    Along the way He trod,
Still learning from all need below
    Depths of the heart of God.

Thy Saviour loves thee

FAR too well thy Saviour loves thee
    To allow thy life to be
One long, calm, unbroken sunbeam,
    One unruffled, stormless sea.

He would have thee fondly nestling
    Closer to His gentle breast,
He would have that world seem brighter,
    Where alone is perfect rest.

Three Needles

A Word to those "Laid Aside"

I HAVE sometimes fancied to myself a comparison between three needles as to their different kinds of work.

First there is the

Mother's Needle.

What a busy life is has! Mending and making, patching and stitching—a button on here, and a tape there. Why, the mother's needle, small though it be, keeps all the house together! "Surely," some might be inclined to say: "no needle *can* have such a useful life as this!"

But there is another needle. It is a

Telegraph Needle.

If you have ever sent off a telegraphic message, you have probably stopped and seen it busy on the dial, working with lightning speed, and ticking off the letters of the messages sent and messages received to and from all parts of the world, as if endowed with life and reason. "Ah!" somebody says: "this is, after all, the most wonderful and the most useful needle in the world!"

Wait a moment, my friend! Here is a ***third*** needle. It is shut up in a little glass cell, all by itself. It cannot work actively, like the mother's needle, as she makes the most of odd minutes to sew and to mend. It does not fly from point to point, like the telegraph needle, every moment carrying important tidings from kings and courts and governments, and from one place to another. Its whole work is that of ***pointing true***. It might say to itself: "What am I doing here, all by myself, and other needles so active? How can a solitary thing like me be of any good?" And yet, millions of lives preserved, ships going from port to port in a safe course, thousands and tens of thousands of homes, to which fathers, husbands, and brothers return in peace from voyages round the world, owe all to that little needle of the

Mariner's Compass,

quivering with intensity in its one work of pointing faithfully to the North Pole.

And so you, dear friend, may be tempted to fancy you can be of little use now. Once, perhaps, you could "do so much"; but your circumstances have changed. Health, openings for usefulness, surroundings of opportunity, are yours no longer, though you long for "active service." But if you are Christ's, remember you can **never** be out of service; and that your work is, in your life, in your words, in your very countenance, to be *pointing true*—pointing all around you to an unseen Saviour, towards whom go out your heart's longings, and who has said: "I, IF I BE LIFTED UP FROM THE EARTH, WILL DRAW ALL MEN UNTO ME!"

If those around you, those in your own home, can discern that you have a Friend whom, not having seen, you love; a Saviour in whom, though now you see Him not, yet believing, you rejoice; if they see that He enables you to suffer cheerfully, to look forward joyfully, to trust in the dark, and at all times, you are doing good service, trained service, bravest service, for your Lord and King—you are **POINTING TRUE.**

On Prayer

"Seek ye My face ... Thy face, Lord, will I seek."—PSALM 27:8
(see also 105:4)

IN prayer I have not only to ask for things, but to *realise the presence* of Him to whom I speak. The power of prayer is gone if I lose the sense of seeing Him by faith. Prayer is not only asking right things, but having the sense of the Person there. If I have not that, I lose the sense of His love, and of being heard.

Samuel Rutherford's Dying Testimony

A FEW days before his death, he said: "I shall shine. I shall see Christ as He is, I shall see Him reign and all His fair company with Him; and I shall have my large share; my eyes shall see my Redeemer; these very eyes of mine, and no other for me. This may seem a wide word, but it is no fancy or delusion; it is true, it is true; let my Lord's name be exalted, and, if He will, let my name be ground to pieces, that He may be *all* in all. If He should slay me ten thousand times ten thousand times, I'll trust."

On another occasion he said: "My eyes shall see my Redeemer, I know He shall stand the last day upon the earth, and I shall be caught up in the clouds to meet Him in the air, and I shall be ever with Him; and what would you have more? *There is an end!*" and, stretching out his hand, again replied: *"There is an end!"* Being asked, "What think you now of Christ?" he answered, "I shall live and adore Him; glory, glory to my Creator and to my Redeemer for ever; glory shines in Immanuel's land." He frequently exclaimed: "Oh, for arms to embrace Him! Oh, for a well-tuned harp!"

On the night of his departure he said: "This night shall close the door and put my anchor within the veil, and I shall go away in a sleep by five o'clock in the morning," which accordingly took place.

When spoken to about his faithfulness in ministering Christ, he said: "I disclaim all that, the port I would be at is Redemption and Forgiveness through His blood; 'Thou wilt show me the path of life, in Thy presence is fulness of joy'; there is nothing now betwixt me and the resurrection; but 'To-day shalt thou be with Me in Paradise.' "

To his child he said: "I have again left you upon the Lord; it may be you will tell this to others, that the lines are fallen to me in pleasant places, I have a goodly heritage; I bless the Lord that gave me counsel."

"Of myself," he said: "I have my own guiltiness, like another sinful man, but *He hath* pardoned, loved, and washed, and given me joy unspeakable and full of glory."

Samuel Rutherford fell asleep in March 1661, repeating the words: "Glory, glory dwelleth in Immanuel's land."

A BRIGHT PROSPECT

WE get too much occupied with **"our LIGHT affliction,"** and **"the moment"** in which it takes place. Our outlook is not far enough, nor high enough, and we are apt to forget the **"far more exceeding and ETERNAL WEIGHT OF GLORY."** The remedy for this is to **"Look ... at the things which are not seen"**—a riddle, a contradiction, a paradox to all but faith, but how blessedly simple to faith.

You have a bright prospect. The most weighty teacher, the most faithful pastor, the most honoured evangelist, has not a brighter prospect than yours. It is to be conformed to the image of God's Son, and spend eternity with Him. **"We know that, when He shall appear, we shall be like Him; for we shall see Him as He is."** Then praise Him **in** the cloud, and soon you will see Him **on** the cloud, to be translated into His presence **without** a cloud.

"Take heed unto thyself"

LET **nothing** come between my soul and God. Keep nothing back from God—tell Him everything as if He knew nothing about it.

Be mercilessly true to yourself, and have everything out with God; none will ever treat you so tenderly as He.

The measure of my love for God's Word is the measure of my love for God; as you reverence Him, so you reverence it.

There is no halting-place short of conformity to Christ; but there is no need to be disheartened, the Holy Spirit is here to work this out in us.

We have a four-fold Strength:—

The Holy Spirit,   **The Word of God,**
The Throne of Grace,   **A Pair of Knees.**

Make use of them: but there is nothing for lazy people.

Take time to pray.

~ ~ ~ ~

Buy the Truth and sell it not. There is a bidder for it—the Devil.

~ ~ ~ ~

Dig into the Word, and meditate upon it. Use your spare moments in the street—anywhere—for meditation. Learn to abstract yourself.

~ ~ ~ ~

Spiritual thinking is what we need; we must work it into our souls. God will reward you. "He that tilleth his land shall have **plenty** of bread." Only that which you appropriate benefits you. (*See Proverbs 12:27*).

~ ~ ~ ~

Is the fear of man before me, or am I satisfied with the private approval of Christ?

~ ~ ~ ~

If you want to get on, keep on praying.

~ ~ ~ ~

Whatever my circumstances are, can I say: "God is love"?

"Take ... no Thought for the Morrow"

READ MATTHEW 6:27-34

ALL one's anxiety cannot add a cubit to the stature, and how much there is in this way for which we are absolutely dependent on the will of Another. Why not then leave all things to Him, to whom we have to leave so much? The weakness of a man's faith is the only really sorrowful weakness after all. And here the Lord appeals to us, whether those who know God are to find His presence with them count for anything or not. The Gentiles away from God, seek after these things as His people do; but we have a Father in heaven who knows our need. We have but to set the heart on His things, and let Him take the burden of ours. Seeking first His kingdom and righteousness, all these things shall be added to us.

Finally, He gives us a limit for care, which by itself would very much exclude it. How much of the burden that we carry belongs really to the morrow—a burden not yet legitimately ours, for who can really tell what shall be on the morrow? Each day will have its own sufficient evil—not too much, for a careful hand has apportioned it; but by borrowing trouble not yet come, we not only necessarily make the burden of the day too heavy, but we cannot reckon upon divine grace for that which is not come, and bear it thus far without assistance. Nay, we have lost Him from our thoughts in all this calculation of the unknown future which is in His hands. How often has love in the most undreamed-of way disappointed all our fears!

"Seek Him that ... turneth the shadow of death into the morning."
Amos 5:8

* * *

"I have chosen thee in the furnace of affliction."
Isaiah 48:10

* * *

"Bread corn is bruised; because He will not ever be threshing it, nor break it with the wheel of His cart, nor bruise it with His horsemen."
Isaiah 28:28

"Before I was afflicted I went astray ... Thou art good, and doest good."
Psalm 119:67-68

* * *

"When thou passest through the waters, I will be with thee; and through the rivers, they shall not overflow thee: when thou walkest through the fire, thou shalt not be burned; neither shall the flame kindle upon thee."
Isaiah 43:2

"Meditate upon these things"

GOD is my only necessity—God is my only resource.

God wants to be everything to every one of us at every moment.

Christianity is **CONformative**, not **REformative**. We belong to an entirely new thing; every particle of power comes from Christ in glory.

God delights in me.

Get God's estimate of God's things, and God's estimate of everything.

Our difficulties should be **food for faith—not** material for failure.

Convert every difficulty into prayer.

If we go through a difficulty with God, all that bound us will be destroyed—*Daniel 3:24 and 25*—and all that is of God will stand.

Delay is not denial. God will come in at the right moment. "My soul, wait thou **only** upon God; for my expectation is from **Him**."

God is behind everything, and there is nothing behind God.

Faith and God see alike. God has Christ before Him—not sin; and faith has the same object as God. *Daniel 3:16-18*—the dignity of faith. "God has not given us the spirit of fear; but of power, and of love, and of a sound mind."

Whatever humbles me, helps me.
　　Not a particle of pride will enter glory. "The proud He knoweth afar off." *Psalm 138:6. See Isaiah 66:2.*

Leave off judging other people, and judge yourself. *Romans 14:12 and 13.*

Set your face in the direction of what you wish to accomplish; and in reading, set your face in the direction of the truth you wish to understand.

Try and **help one another** on for Eternity; and let **nothing** come in to hinder **prayer**.

"O taste and see that the Lord **is** good."

Extracts

❈ ❈

To true happiness here, as well as for a guard against the dangers of it, some strain of sorrow seems of necessity to mingle with it, something wherein the soul has to submit itself to God—to say: "It is the Lord."

❈ ❈ ❈

Our joy to be solid must rest on something immovable. Just as soon as we hang our happiness on circumstances or surroundings, we go up or we go down with the tide. The thermometer of our joy is at the mercy of outside circumstances. "REJOICE IN THE LORD ALWAY: AND AGAIN I SAY, REJOICE."

❈ ❈ ❈

You may be sure of this, that God never sent a trial so bitter that a Christ-filled Christian could not suck some honey out of it. God does not expect us to be callous under trial, or ask us to make merry at a funeral. But away down, deep under the tempest of trial He gives us a serene sense that whatever He does is right.

❈ ❈ ❈

Oh! the power and the joy of being nothing, having nothing, and knowing nothing but a glorified Christ up there in heaven; and of being "careful for nothing" but the honour of His precious Name down here on earth.

Sometime, Somewhere

UNANSWERED yet? the prayer your lips have pleaded
In agony of heart these many years?
Doth faith begin to fail, is faith departing,
And think you all in vain these falling tears?
Say not the Father hath NOT heard your prayer,
You shall have your desire sometime, somewhere.

Unanswered yet? though when you first presented
This one petition at the Father's throne,
It seemed as though it could not wait the asking,
So urgent was the heart to make it known.
Though years have passed since then, do NOT despair,
The Lord will answer you, sometime, somewhere.

Unanswered yet? Nay, do not say ungranted;
Perhaps YOUR part is not yet wholly done—
The work began when first your prayer was uttered,
And God will finish what He has begun.
If you will keep the incense burning—prayer,
His glory you shall see sometime, somewhere.

Unanswered yet? Faith CANNOT be unanswered;
Her feet are firmly planted on the Rock,
Amid the wildest storms she stands undaunted,
Nor quails beneath the loudest thunder shock.
She KNOWS Omnipotence has heard her prayer;
And cries: "It shall be done sometime, somewhere."

The Lord of Hosts and the God of Jacob

"The Lord of hosts is with us; the God of Jacob is our refuge." (Psalm 46)

TWICE over in this Psalm do we get these remarkable words: "The Lord of hosts is with us; the God of Jacob is our refuge"—a Psalm, too, for the sons of rebellious Korah. It is like the wonderful refrain: "For His mercy endureth for ever," occurring again and again in the Old Testament, and repeated twenty-six times in the twenty-six verses of Psalm 136—a mercy that nothing can exhaust or break down, a mercy that endureth FOR EVER.

"The Lord of Hosts!"

What a comforting expression! How it stills our hearts in the presence of all the power of the enemy! "The Lord of hosts," whose unlimited power and boundless resources make the victory certain. And if we can complete the sentence, however feeble and weak, we may well remain in perfect peace. "The Lord of hosts IS WITH US." Absolutely feeble, absolutely weak—it matters not. "The Lord of hosts IS WITH US." That settles everything.

No wonder the Psalmist, with less light than ourselves, could triumphantly exclaim:—

"God is our refuge and strength,
A very present help in trouble.
Therefore will not we fear, though the earth be removed,
And though the mountains be carried into the midst of
  the sea;
Though the waters thereof roar and be troubled,
Though the mountains shake with the swelling thereof.
Selah!"

Well might he pause (Selah!) at this point. What more suggestive of stability than the earth we walk upon and the everlasting hills? What more emblematical of instability than the restless sea? Yet when the most unstable thing overcomes the most stable, when the mountains are carried into the midst of the sea, the Psalmist has something immovable on which to rest—

God is our refuge and help.

Restless, troubled child of God, do you thus know "the Lord of hosts"? Do you think the power of evil can ever conquer God or thwart His purposes of love? Nay, how can you doubt for one moment?

The Psalmist knew "the Lord of hosts." That was enough to deliver him from every tempest of fear. But we can go a step further. A step?—ay, many steps.

We know God as Father.

He numbers the hairs of our head. He puts our tears in the bottle of His remembrance.

> *"Precious thought, my Father knoweth,*
>   *Careth for His child;*
> *Bids me nestle closer to Him*
>   *When the storm beats wild.*
> *Though my earthly hopes are shattered,*
>   *And the teardrops fall,*
> *Yet He is Himself my solace,*
>   *Yea, my 'all in all.'"*

When "the Lord of hosts is with us" we can be at peace in the midst of the storm, but when in spirit we are with Him, we are where the storms come not. What a change!—from the waters roaring and troubled, and the mountains shaking, to the peace that surrounds Him. We read in the next verse—

"There is a river, the streams whereof shall make glad the city of God,
The holy place of the tabernacles of the Most High.
God is in the midst of her; she shall not be moved."

What a contrast! We are across the bar of the open tempestuous sea, and have reached the calm, sweet haven of rest. The storm and the raging waters are exchanged for the river of God—calm, peaceful, gladdening, refreshing!

Doubtless this refers to an earthly Jerusalem—an earthly millennium. But can we not transfer the simile, and put it in the setting of Christianity? Do we not know what it is to leave our own tumultuous circumstances and make a journey in spirit into that region where the river of His pleasure flows, where there is no trail of the serpent, no blight, no sin, no death, no unsatisfied longing?

The storms but drive us nearer home, and the discipline of a Father's hand may all be turned to account. But how blessed to anticipate the peace of home, to drink even now of the river of His pleasure, ere we reach it and know it in all its blessed fulness and reality!

But the Psalmist goes on—

"He maketh wars to cease unto the end of the earth;
He breaketh the bow, and cutteth the spear in sunder;
He burneth the chariot in the fire.
Be still, and know that I am God."

For the present God is our refuge; in the future He will subdue all the power of the enemy, and the whole earth shall be at rest. Let US learn our lesson: "Be STILL, and know that I am God."

"The God of Jacob"

Why not the God of ISRAEL? "The Lord of hosts" gives us the sense of His power; "the God of JACOB" tells us the kind of people He shows mercy to, and the omnipotence of that mercy. None but God could have gone on with Jacob, and at the last brought him to worship as, in the weakness of death, he leant upon his staff.

"The God of JACOB." How it appeals to us, for we are all Jacobs! Scheming, plotting, covetous man! As Jacob there is nothing, absolutely nothing to commend him. He took advantage of his brother's dire need to deprive him of his birthright. He deceived his blind old father to secure it. His aftercourse was marked by intrigue and weakness. And yet the Psalmist at a later date could write: "The God of Jacob is our refuge."

Was it that God condoned Jacob's plotting and wickedness? Far be the thought. And if we find, even as Christians, the tendency to evil within and constant failure that only our God knows, is it that He can go on with sin? We may be outwardly irreproachable in conduct, but how many, nay, all of us, mourn over our weakness and inconsistency! How, then, can God be the God of Jacob—OUR God?

Is it not that He breaks down the Jacob in us? Do not we all halt upon our thighs more or less? Step by step, God weakened Jacob till at length, in the very weakness of death, he could, leaning on his staff, worship.

And so "the God of Jacob" deals with us. The flesh has been unsparingly judged at the cross, and His mercy endureth for ever, for He takes steps that Jacob shall practically die. We may not die physically, but just in proportion as the Jacob within us is held to be dead or we dead to it, so are we ready to worship.

May we trust "the Lord of hosts" more—may we submit to the ways of "the God of Jacob" with us, and blessing will result. What a God is ours! How perfect are His ways!

∽ "THE LIGHT THAT FAILED" ∽

WHAT wonderful ways can God use to bless and refresh His weary ones! Who would ever dream of the flaring advertisement of a play upon the hoarding being employed as a messenger of God! Yet one, who had suffered sore bereavement caught sight of these words, and blessed God for the light that NEVER fails. Earthly light, be it health or the joy of friends, or the love of husband or wife or parent or child, will fail, but the Christian has a portion that never faileth.

Saul of Tarsus was converted by that "light from heaven, above the brightness of the sun," controlled by it, comforted by it and he found it indeed the light that never failed. It is in hours of deepest darkness that it shines with its brightest and most inward light in our hearts. "The path of the just shineth more and more unto the perfect day." Oh! for more of that blessed shining.

Thou Knowest
Psalm 56:8; 107:4-7

GOD over all, most blessed now and ever,
  Thou tell'st my wand'rings, markest out my life;
And no wild storm, nor blast of pain, shall sever
  My soul from Thee amid the billows' strife.

Not as a straw toss'd on the waves of sorrow,
  Nor on a desert that hath ne'er a way,
Thou know'st my past, my present, and my morrow,
  Thou tell'st my wand'rings here, from day to day.

Of love Thou art the largest, truest Giver;
  Thy sympathies flow ever full and free;
Thy peace, O God, is like a deep, calm river,
  Whose currents bear me to Thy home and Thee.

And if the road that leads me to Thy dwelling
  Be called by Thee "A solitary way,"
Thy light shall shine, its darkness all dispelling,
  Still more and more until the perfect day.

Not as one desolate I tread life's pathway;
  The Servant* leads me, journey'ng to Thy Son;
The day is nearing when His patient mission,
  And all His gracious guidings shall be done.

The moment when He says, "It is my Master,"
  With veiled heart I speed me on to hear;
With energies aroused, I press on faster,
  For in the twilight, He Himself draws near!

*Genesis 24: 61-65.

In the Hand of God

HIDDEN in the hollow
  Of His blessed Hand,
Never foe can follow,
  Never traitor stand;
Not a surge of worry,
  Not a shade of care,
Not a blast of hurry
  Touch the spirit there.

EVERY joy or trial
  Falleth from above,
Traced upon our dial
  By the Sun of Love.
We may trust Him solely
  All for us to do;
They who trust Him wholly
  Find Him wholly true.

Now and Hereafter

*"What I do thou knowest not now;
but thou shalt know hereafter."—John 13:7.*

THESE words of our Lord, as we all know, refer to His washing the feet of His disciples. Behind that lowly act a hidden meaning lay which should be made quite plain to them one day. So when the work of redemption was accomplished, and Christ had taken His seat on high, and the Holy Spirit had come down, many a mystery was made clear, and many a thing told out that could not be told before.

But we are going to deal with these words in other connections now. Many a dear child of God is walking in a rough and rugged road, and passing through circumstances hard to understand. He sees no reason why he should be dealt with thus. With anxious heart he looks up and asks, "Lord, why is it thus with me?" And the answer is, "What I do thou knowest not now; but thou shalt know hereafter." With this he must be satisfied, and wait with patience the clearing of the clouds.

For example, the little home at Bethany, where Jesus was always welcome, had been thrown into great sorrow (*John 11*). Lazarus was sick. Now "Lazarus" means "GOD MY HELPER." To whom, therefore, should they turn in their distress but to Him who had come so near to them in grace? Short was the message which the sisters sent: "LORD, BEHOLD, HE WHOM THOU LOVEST IS SICK." And there was every reason to believe that the Lord would hasten to their relief. For Jesus loved Lazarus, and if earthly love delights to do its best, what would not the love of Jesus do? So everything encouraged them to look for an early deliverance. Yet it did not come! Their expectations were not fulfilled. The sisters' message was received, but after the swift feet of the messenger had departed Jesus abode "two days" in the same place where He was. This delay must have sorely tried their hearts, nor could they divine a reason for it. And all the while Lazarus grew worse, and grim death knocked loudly at the door. In vain they looked for Jesus. He did not come, and their flickering hopes were finally extinguished when their brother breathed his last. Nevertheless, though they knew it not, His hand was all the time upon the helm, steering the ship aright. In the whirlwind and in the storm He has His way, and the clouds from which they shrank were but the sure sign that He was near, for they were "the dust of His feet." (*Nahum 1:3*).

"What I do thou knowest not now; but thou shalt know hereafter" are words which might have been well addressed to the dear friends at Bethany in their most anxious hours. Their confidence in the love of Jesus was possibly unshaken, but this long and fatal delay was most perplexing. Could they, did they believe that all things were working together for good? that every detail was under the control of One who never erred, and whose love for them was deeper than the sea? We cannot tell. "Lord, if Thou hadst been here my brother had not died," are words which seem to come from hearts not quite submissive and at rest. But when the "HERE-AFTER" came, and the purpose of God in this sickness was fulfilled, and Lazarus was given back to his sisters, and the glory of God and of Him who was the Resurrection and the Life was seen in cloudless and broadened vision, then how gladly would they have owned that God's way was perfect, and that blessed is the man whose hope in Him is steadfast!

"Satisfied the way He taketh
Must be always best."

And we may look at Paul, too, after he had been caught up into Paradise, where he heard unspeakable words and received visions and revelations of the Lord (*2 Corinthians 12*). Such high privilege exposed him to a subtle snare, which at the time he did not see, but which the Lord knew, and from which He would save His faithful servant at all costs. For this "a thorn in the flesh" was needful. There have been many conjectures as to what the thorn was, but they are only conjectures at their best, and therefore of no value. God has not told us, so it is not necessary that we should know. But it was something hard to bear—as men speak—and which Paul earnestly prayed might be taken away. "What I do thou knowest not now; but thou shalt know hereafter," is a saying which applies to such a case as his. Think of that, dear saint and devoted servant of Christ! Think of him as he bows his knees to the Lord, and asks in fervent prayer that this distressing infirmity might depart from him! But no answer came though he may have long and patiently waited for it. Again he prays, and again no answer. For the third time he prays, then the silence is broken, the tarrying time is over, the suspense is ended, and the answer comes. But there is no taking away of the thorn—THAT is left to rankle, to be felt always, and always to be endured with pain and patience. The answer to Paul's cry came in a form which was better than the removal of the distressing thing: "AND HE SAID UNTO ME, MY GRACE IS SUFFICIENT FOR THEE: FOR MY STRENGTH IS MADE PERFECT IN WEAKNESS."

Shall we, then, think it strange if the Lord's way with us is at times after the same order, though the pattern of it may be different? Have we prayed for deliverance, and as yet no hand has been stretched out to deliver? It is the tarrying time, the "two days" of the Bethany story. Alas! with many of us these testing times show that our faith is but a slender plank that will bear but little strain. Let none of us think that the Lord has forgotten us. A mother may forget her child, but He will not forget us. Our names are ever before Him, graven on the palms of those hands once pierced for us at Calvary. The present moment may be the "NOW" when we know not; tomorrow may be the "HEREAFTER" when we shall fully know our Master's end and aim.

And if, as in Paul's case, the answer to our oft-repeated cry comes not in the way of deliverance; if instead of removing the trying thing, He speaks to our hearts in tender, gracious power, saying, "My grace is sufficient for thee," shall we not bow submissively to His perfect will, assured that His choice is wiser and better than ours? May we not even go further, as Paul did when he said, "Most gladly, therefore, will I rather glory in my infirmities, that the power of Christ may rest upon me"? It is a great thing to say, for GLORYING in our infirmities goes far beyond bearing them with patience and submission. But His grace enables His weak and suffering saints thus to speak when He is fully trusted and His will accepted in perfect acquiescence. We rest, then, as one rests on a bed of down, and we gladly leave ourselves in His hands as we hear Him say, "What I do thou knowest not now; but thou shalt know hereafter."

> # HIS APPOINTMENT
>
> "DISAPPOINTMENT—His appointment,"
> Change one letter, then I see
> That the thwartings of my purpose
> Is God's BETTER choice for me.
> His appointment MUST be blessing
> Tho' it MAY come in disguise,
> For the end from the beginning
> Open to His wisdom lies.

A Few Thoughts on Psalm 23 and John 10

Psalm 23 is the sheep speaking about the Shepherd; John 10 the Shepherd speaking about His sheep. In the former, although the writer was inspired by the Holy Ghost, David's experience of the Shepherd must necessarily have been limited. In the latter the Good Shepherd knows all about His sheep perfectly, knows what poor wandering things we are, and in spite of it speaks of our not perishing, and having eternal life! How wonderful! What ample provision He has made for His own!

But there are two negatives in Psalm 23 lying like two precious glittering gems amid all the positive blessings that David enumerates:

"**I shall not want.**" (*Verse 1*).
"**I will fear no evil.**" (*Verse 4*).

If I do not want in the *present*, and do not fear for the *future*, then surely I am in a happy position.

David himself had been a shepherd, and as a king he was called to shepherd Jehovah's people, and he knew something of what it meant. If he could say the Lord is my Shepherd, "I shall not want" was a necessary deduction.

And the careful observer of the two Scriptures will be able to trace in Psalm 23 all the blessings that the Good Shepherd tells us about in John 10, perhaps dimly and obscurely, but still there. Not, of course, in all the full light and relationship of Christianity, but still there in a Jewish mould. All this is deeply interesting and instructive and comforting. We can read Psalm 23 in the light of John 10.

The Touch of Jesus

"And Jesus came and touched them, and said, 'Arise, and be not afraid.'"

HE touched my restless heart, and all was still,
And I was just content to wait His will;
He told me how I yet should surely see
That He had planned the very best for me—
Could I not trace His love in all the past?
Well might I know all would be right at last.
Ah! blessed, soothing touch! 'Tis His, I know,
No other hand could ever touch me so;
The longings, and the achings, and the pain,
But meet that touch, and all is calm again.
He touched me first, when I was full of sin,
For I have heard Him saying, "Be thou clean,"
And then He touched my eyes that I might see
His beauty, which eclipsed all else for me.
Without His tender touch, my hands by turn
Hang idle, or with restless fever burn;
That touch alone can loose the speechless tongue,
So that His endless praises may be sung.
And so I need His touches, day by day,
Earth's fevers, and earth's fears, to take away;
To bid the wonderings, and the doubtings cease,
And fill me with His own unclouded peace.

Settled Peace

THE moment we begin to rest our peace on anything in ourselves, we lose it, and this is why so many saints have not settled peace.

Nothing can be lasting that is not built on God alone.

How can you have settled peace? Only by having it in God's own way, by not resting on anything, even the Spirit's work within yourselves, but on what Christ has done entirely without you. Then you will know peace, conscious unworthiness, but yet peace. In Christ alone, God finds that in which He can rest; and so it is with His saints. The more you see of the extent and nature of the evil that is within as well as that without and around, the more you will find that what Jesus is and did is the only ground at all on which you can rest.

❋ "Who shall roll away the Stone?" ❋
—— Mark 16:3 ——

WHAT poor weeping ones were saying
    Nineteen hundred years ago,
We, the same weak faith betraying,
    Say in our sad hours of woe;
Looking at some trouble lying
    In the dark and dread unknown,
We too often ask with sighing:
    "Who shall roll away the stone?"

Thus with care our spirits crushing
    When they should from care be free,
And in spirit, soul out-gushing,
    Rise in rapture, Lord, to Thee.
For before the day was ended,
    Oft we've had with joy to own
Angels have from heaven descended
    And have rolled away the stone.

Many a storm-cloud hov'ring o'er us
    Never pours on us its rain;
Many a grief we see before us
    Never comes to cause us pain.
Oft-times, on the dread to-morrow
    Sunshine comes, the cloud has flown!
Why then ask in foolish sorrow:
    "Who shall roll away the stone?"

Burden not thy soul with sadness,
    Make a wiser, better choice,
Drink the wine of Life with gladness,
    God doth bid thee, Saint, rejoice!
In to-day's bright sunlight basking
    Leave to-morrow's cares alone;
Spoil not present joys by asking:
    "Who shall roll away the stone?"

✷ THE POWER OF ✷
THE CROSS OF CHRIST

✷ ✷ ✷ ✷ ✷

THEY were living to themselves: self, with its hopes, and promises, and dreams, had still hold of them; but He began to fulfil their prayers. They had asked for contrition, and He sent them sorrow; they had asked for purity, and He sent them thrilling anguish; they had asked to be meek, and He had broken their hearts; they had asked to be dead to the world, and He slew all their living hopes; they had asked to be made like unto Him, and He placed them in the furnace, sitting by "as a refiner of silver" till they should reflect His image. They had asked to lay hold of His cross, and when He had reached it to them it lacerated their hands; they had asked they knew not what, nor how; but He had taken them at their word, and granted them all their petitions.

They were hardly willing to follow on so far, or to draw so nigh to Him. They had upon them an awe and fear, as Jacob at Bethel, or Eliphaz in the night visions, or as the apostles when they thought they had seen a spirit, and knew not that it was Jesus: they could almost pray Him to depart from them, or to hide His awfulness. They found it easier to obey than to suffer—to do than to give up—to bear the cross than to hang upon it; but they cannot go back, for they have come too near the unseen cross, and its virtues have pierced too deeply within them. He is fulfilling to them His promise: "And I, if I be lifted up, will draw all men unto Me"; but now THEIR turn is come at last, and that is all.

Before, they had only HEARD of the mystery, but now they FEEL it. He had fastened on them His look of love, as He did on Mary and Peter, and they cannot choose but follow. Little by little, from time to time, by flitting gleams, the mystery of His cross shines out upon them. They behold Him, and lifted up, and the glory which rays forth from the wounds of His holy passion; and as they gaze upon Him they advance, and are changed into His likeness, and His Name shines out through them, for He dwells in them. They live alone with Him above, in unspeakable fellowship: willing to lack what others own, and to be unlike all, so that they are only like Him.

Such are they in all ages who follow the Lamb whithersoever He goeth. Had they chosen for themselves, or their friends chosen for them, they would have chosen otherwise. They would have been brighter here, but less glorious in His kingdom. They would have had Lot's portion, not Abraham's, if they had halted anywhere—if He had taken off His hand and let them stray back—and what would they not have lost? What forfeits in the morning of the resurrection! But He staid them up, even against themselves. Many a time their foot had well-nigh slipped. But He in mercy held them up; now, even in this life, they know all He did was done well. It was good for them to stand alone with Him, on the mountain and in the cloud, and that not their will, but His, was done on them.

❋ ❋ ❋ ❋ ❋

The Glory of that Light

I WAS journeying in the noontide,
    When His light shone o'er my road—
And I saw Him in that glory,
    Saw Him—JESUS, Son of God.
All around, in noontide splendour,
    Earthly scenes lay fair and bright,
But my eyes no longer see them
    For the Glory of that Light.

Others in the summer sunshine,
    Wearily may journey on—
I have seen a light from heaven
    Past the brightness of the sun,
Light that knows no cloud, no waning,
    Light wherein I see His face,
All His love's uncounted treasures,
    All the riches of His grace.

All the wonders of His glory,
    Deeper wonders of His love,
How for me He won—He keepeth
    That high place in heaven above.
Not a glimpse—the veil uplifted,
    But within the veil to dwell
Gazing on His face for ever,
    Hearing words unspeakable.

Marvel not that Christ in glory
    All my inmost heart hath won,
Not a star to cheer my darkness,
    But a light beyond the sun.
All below lies dark and shadowed,
    Nothing there to rest my heart,
Save the lonely track of sorrow
    Where of old He walked apart.

I have seen the face of Jesus—
    Tell me not of aught beside;
I have heard the voice of Jesus—
    All my soul is satisfied.
In the radiance of the glory
    First I saw His blessed face,
And for ever shall that glory
    Be my home—my resting-place.

God Knows Best

GOD would never send you the darkness,
   If He felt you could bear the light;
   But you would not cling to His guiding hand,
If the way were always bright:
And you would not care to walk by faith,
   Could you always walk by sight.

'Tis true He has many an anguish
   For your sorrowful heart to bear,
And many a cruel thorn-crown
   For your tired head to wear;
He knows how few could reach heaven at all,
   If pain did not drive them there.

So He sends you this blinding darkness,
   And this furnace of seven-fold heat;
'Tis the only way, believe me,
   To keep you close to His feet;
For 'tis always so easy to wander,
   When our lives are glad and sweet.

Then nestle your hand in your Father's,
   And sing, if you can, as you go;
Your song may cheer some one behind you,
   Whose courage is sinking low,
And well if your lips do quiver,
   God will love it better so.

A Word to Doubters

Read *carefully* John 3:36 and 5:24, and Acts 13:38-39.

IF all the *shalls* in Scripture meant *perhaps*,
   And all the *haths* meant simply *hope to have*,
And all the *ares* depended on an *if*,
        I well might doubt;
But since our Saviour-God means what He says,
        And cannot lie,
I trust His faithful word, and *know* that I
Shall surely dwell throughout eternity
With Him whose love led Him for me to die,
        E'en Christ Himself.

Particularly note the words *is* and *Verily, verily,* in the above text uttered by the blessed Saviour. Also notice that the word *know* occurs forty-two times in John's Epistles, which are addressed to *believers* in the Lord Jesus Christ.

Unveiled Mysteries

"What I do thou knowest not now; but thou shalt know hereafter."

MUCH is baffling and perplexing to us in God's present dealings. "What!" we are often ready to exclaim, "could not the cup have been less bitter—the trial less severe—the road less rough and dreary?" Hush thy misgivings, says a gracious God; arraign not the rectitude of My dispensations. Thou shalt yet see all revealed and made bright in the mirror of eternity. What I do—it is all My doing, My appointment. Thou hast but a partial view of these dealings; thou canst see nought but plans crossed and gourds laid low. But I see the end from the beginning.

"Who is wise, and he shall understand these things? prudent, and he shall know them? for the ways of the Lord are right, and the just shall walk in them."

"Fear Not"

O thou of dark forebodings drear,
  O thou of such a faithless heart,
Hast thou forgotten what thou art,
  That thou hast ventured so to fear?

No weed art thou on ocean cast,
  Borne by its never-resting foam
This way and that, without a home,
  Till flung on some bleak shore at last:

But thou the lotus, which above,
  Swayed here and there by wind and tide,
Yet still below doth fixed abide,
  Fast rooted in Eternal Love.

❋ ❋ ❋ ❋

THE BURDEN OF PRAYER

LORD, what a change within us one short hour
  Spent in Thy presence will prevail to make,
What heavy burdens from our bosoms take,
What parched grounds refresh as with a shower!
We kneel, and all around us seems to lower;
We rise, and all—the distant and the near—
Stands forth in sunny outline, brave and clear;
We kneel how weak; we rise how full of power.
Why therefore should we do ourselves this wrong
Or others—that we are not always strong,
That we are ever overborne with care,
That we should ever weak or heartless be,
Anxious or troubled, when with us is prayer,
And joy and strength and courage are with Thee?

Everlasting Love

"I have loved thee with an Everlasting Love"

BELIEVER, art thou now tempted to doubt His love? Are His footsteps lost amid the night shadows, through which He is now conducting thee? What appears to thee now some capricious exercise of His power or sovereignty is the determination and decree of everlasting love. He seems to say, "I loved thee, suffering one, into this affliction; I will love thee through it, and when My designs regarding thee are completed, I will show that the love, which is from everlasting is to everlasting."

Child of God! If there be a ripple now agitating the surface of the stream, trace it up to this fountain-head of love.

The Permanent and the Passing Away
❋ ❋ ❋ ❋ ❋

DOUBTING and inconsistency and unbelief are but passing away. Sorrow and pain and trial are not permanent. A few more turns of the clock and swings of the pendulum, and then farewell for ever to sin and failures. Farewell to doubts and fears—a final farewell. We are to be conformed to the image of His Son. We shall be ushered into the reign of light and of eternal realities. Then goodbye FAITH. Farewell HOPE. I am launched out into one great eternal sea of love. FAITH and HOPE make very good companions on the road, but not for eternity. They go with us to the gate, but LOVE is inside. GOD is LOVE. We shall be plunged into the ocean of love, lost in it, never to come out. It is shoreless, bottomless, and infinite. We shall soon be in a region where we shall know as known, and there will not be a thought or a feeling, which will be unlike Christ. No trouble or sorrow, all will have for ever passed away. The first thousand years in glory will roll along with Hallelujah to the LAMB! Another thousand comes, and we are still praising the Lord together. The pendulum of praise never ceases to swing. He will be the object of our adoring praise and worship for ever. Eternity! Eternity! Eternity! How long art thou? Not too long to gaze on the LAMB. Then the PERMANENT. Nothing but CHRIST—the CHRIST of GOD, for ever, for ever, and for ever. *Amen.*

Cleave to the Lord

❈ ❈ ❈ ❈ ❈

CLEAVE to the Lord with purpose of heart. Depend on Him. There is power in Christ; there is sufficiency in Christ for all He would have you do or be. Some are allowed a long season of joy on first believing. But God knows our hearts, and how soon we begin to depend on our joy, and not on Christ. HE is our object—not the joy.

Sin no longer remains ON you, but the flesh is IN you to the end: the old stock will put forth its buds, which must be nipped off as they appear. No fruit can come of it. It is the new nature that bears fruit UNTO GOD. But though the flesh is in you, do not be thinking of this, THINK OF CHRIST.

As you grow in the knowledge of Christ, a joy comes, deeper than the first joy. I have known Christ more or less between thirty and forty years, and I can truly say I have ten thousand times more joy in Him now than I had at first. It is a deeper, calmer joy. The water rushing down a hill is beautiful to look at, and makes most noise; but you will find the water in the plain deeper, calmer, more fit for general use.

Cleave to Christ with purpose of heart. A distracted heart is the bane of Christians. When we have got something that is not Christ, we are away from the source of strength. When my soul is FILLED with Christ, I have no heart or eye for the trash of this world. If Christ is dwelling in your heart by faith, it will not be a question with you: "What harm is there in this and that?" But rather, "Am I doing this for Christ?" "Can Christ go along with me in this?"

Do not let the world come in and distract your thoughts. I speak especially to you young ones. They who are older have had more experience in it, and know more what it is worth: but it all lies shining before you, endeavouring to attract you. Its smiles are deceitful; still it smiles. It makes promises which it cannot keep; still it makes them. Your hearts are too big for the world; it cannot fill them. They are too little for Christ: He fills heaven, He will fill you to overflowing. "WITH PURPOSE OF HEART ... cleave unto the Lord." He knew how treacherous the heart is, and how soon it would put anything in HIS place. You will have indeed to learn what is in your own heart.

Abide with God, and you will learn it with Him, and with His grace. If you do not, you will have to learn it with bitter sorrow, through the successful temptation of the devil. But God is faithful. If you have been getting away from Him, and other things have come in, and formed a crust, as it were, over your hearts, you will not at once get back the joy. God will have you deal with this crust, and get rid of it.

Remember Christ bought you with His own blood, that you should be His, not the world's. Do not let Satan get between you and God's grace. However careless you may have been, however far you may have got away from Him, count on His love. It is His joy to see you back again. Look at the sin with horror, but never wrong Him by distrusting His love. Mistrust not His work, mistrust not His love. He has loved you, and will love you to the end. Talk much with Jesus. Never be content without being able to walk and talk with Christ as with a dear friend. Be not satisfied with anything short of close intercourse of soul with Him who has loved you and washed you from your sins in His own blood.

"Step by Step"

A DOCTOR was once asked by a patient who had met with a serious accident, "Doctor, how long shall I have to lie here?" The answer, **"Only a day at a time,"** taught the patient a precious lesson.

The same lesson God taught His people, and the people of all ages since, through the method of His provision for Israel during their wilderness journey. "The day's portion in its day" (Exodus 16:4, margin). Day by day the manna fell, enough for each day, and no more and no less.

So God promises us, not "As thy **weeks**," or "As thy **months**," but "As thy **DAYS**, so shall thy strength be." And that means Monday's grace for Monday, and Tuesday's grace for Tuesday, and so on. Why, then, borrow trouble for the future? We are especially told by the Lord to "take no thought for **to-morrow**." The true rule is to live by the day, to live a life of trust.

The law of Divine grace is, "Sufficient unto **the day**." The law of Divine deliverance is, "A very **present** help." The law of Divine guidance is, **"Step by step."**

One who carries a lantern on a dark road at night sees only a step before him. If he takes that step he carries the lantern forward and that makes another step plain. At length he reaches his destination in safety without once stepping into darkness. The whole way was made light to him, though only a single step of it was made plain at one time. This is the method of God's guidance—one step at a time.

It is a blessed secret, this of living by the day. Anyone can carry his burden, however heavy, till nightfall. Anyone can do his work, however hard, for one day. And in the strength of God, anyone can live trustingly, lovingly, and purely till the sun goes down. And this is all that life really means to us—just one little day.

"Day by day the manna fell;
Oh! to learn this lesson well."

A Psalm of Silence

"My soul is silent upon God."—*Psalm 62:1* [Marginal reading]

TOO weak to think, Lord!
   Too weak to pray!
  Too weak for song of praise:
    Yet still I say,
"Now draw Thou near, Lord;
Banish all fear, Lord;
Let me in quiet hear
    Thy voice to-day!"

I would not ask, Lord,
    What shall befall;
Only the loving past
    Silent recall;
Jesus the lost one sought,
Jesus my soul hath bought;
This calms each troubled thought,
    This answers all.

Therefore I leave to Thee
    What shall betide;
One word enough for me—
    Jesus has died.
He for His weak one pleads,
He on to glory leads,
He knows my cares, my needs,
    He will provide.

Too weak to think, Lord!
    Too weak to pray!
Yet from my heart of hearts
    Silent I say,
"Do Thou Thy will, Lord:
Keep Thou me still, Lord,
And heart and spirit fill
    With peace to-day!"

A Letter

DEAR TRIED FRIEND,

You are unknown to me, but the same blessed Master that cheered me in times of deep, deep trial will comfort you. Every hair of your head is numbered, and the common house sparrow reminds us daily of our Father's care, for the sight of it recalls those marvellous words that fell from the Master's lips: **"Are not five sparrows sold for two farthings, and not one of them is forgotten before God? Ye are of more value than many sparrows."** (*Luke 12:6-7*). In another Gospel we read that **two** sparrows were sold for **one** farthing, so that if **five** were sold for **two** farthings, it means that they were of such little value that one was thrown in to tempt the purchaser. Yet God, so great that nothing is too great for Him, and so great that nothing is too small, marks the falling sparrow. What comfort in this! Nay more, the whole truth of a Father's love and care could not come out till after the ascension of the Lord, and **now** we know that we are God's children. How, then, can there be the least question as to His love and power? "BEHOLD, WHAT MANNER OF LOVE."

I know that bodily infirmity brings us very low sometimes—mental affliction or nervous troubles are very real, but the Lord knows all about it. I have known trouble to take such a hold upon me, that I have cried out like Peter, when he was sinking in the water: "Lord, save me." But once we get into His presence, we find His high priestly hand stretched out to support us, where nature and common sense would say it were impossible.

Job with his little light, and at best but a **servant** of God, whilst you and I are His **children**, often puts me to shame. He said: "THOUGH HE SLAY ME, YET WILL I TRUST IN HIM." (*Job 13:15*). True, he did not know himself, for he boasted in the next breath of his own integrity; but at any rate he had a sublime confidence in God. He was tried as no one has ever been. At one stroke, reduced from being the richest sheik in the East, to poverty; at the same time not one child, but all his sons and daughters swept away; then his body afflicted, not with an ordinary visitation, but from sole to crown with sore boils. Sitting in the dust with his three friends aggravating him, one is more and more astonished at his words. With our God-given knowledge of a Father's heart, and in the light of the cross, can we repine? Surely not. Then let us praise Him, though it be with trembling voice.

Yours affectionately in the Lord,

* * * *

"Rest at Noon"

"Tell me, O Thou whom my soul loveth, where Thou feedest, where Thou makest Thy flock to rest at noon: for why should I be as one that turneth aside by the flocks of Thy companions?"

Song of Solomon 1:7.

"REST at noon"! How inviting it sounds! The song we have culled the expression from is rich in Oriental images. To gain some idea of the simile we must transport ourselves in imagination to Eastern lands. It is noon, and the rays of the scorching sun are beating upon the parched and wearied earth. There is no escape from its pitiless glare. But there is One in our passage who is skilful in finding rest even at noon for His flock. He is addressed as the One "whom my soul loveth."

Dear troubled, anxious Christian, let me apply the simile to what you know something of. Has it been noon with you? Have the scorching rays of tribulation, of trial, of weakness of body, of shattered hopes and broken spirit reached you, till you have felt you could not bear more? *What you need is* **REST**.

There is One, whom thy soul loveth, who can give it. That One loves you well, and He it is who has given you the tribulation, the weakness of body, the broken spirit in order that, parched and weary, you might at length turn to Him and find "rest at noon." There is a spot even then of perfect rest. What a rest it is! To lie perfectly passive in His hands, knowing that **The Love**, the perfect divine love, which has planned out your pathway, has measured in its omniscience the weight of your sorrow. He is engaged in working out the purposes of His love in you for His own glory first, and then for your exceeding gain. In the knowledge of that love your heart may rest— "REST AT NOON."

I knew a Christian who was dying. One would have thought that he could not stand any greater pressure and further weakening, but the fiercer the rays the more beautiful was the rest that he enjoyed. There is no possible combination of circumstances in which this rest may not be known.

"A MAN shall be ... as the shadow of a great rock in a weary land." (*Isaiah 32:2*).

"Come unto ME, all ye that labour and are heavy laden, and I will give you rest." (*Matthew 11:28*).

The same truth is put in different ways. In all our weariness we know Him, who knew weariness and thirst—**A Man**, verily, "God over all, blessed for ever," yet truly **Man**, now glorified, the Succourer of His people, their great High Priest, "touched with the feeling of our infirmities." Surely we can find rest in Him, as under "the shadow of a great rock in a weary land." Ay, and He gives the invitation: "Come UNTO ME, all ye that labour and are heavy laden, and I will give you rest"—an invitation most blessedly falling from the lips of the Gospel preacher; and no weary sinner who comes to Him, but will find rest, yet not confined to that, but an invitation to *you* that labour and are heavy laden to rest.

Blessed Jesus! The One whom our souls love is He who can give rest to His flock at noon. "REST AT NOON"! Do you know anything of it?

Last Words of Samuel Rutherford

✳ ✳ ✳ ✳ ✳

"Glory—Glory dwelleth
in Immanuel's Land"

The sands of time are sinking,
  The dawn of heaven breaks,
The summer morn I've sighed for,
  The fair sweet morn awakes:
Dark, dark hath been the midnight,
  But dayspring is at hand,
And glory—glory dwelleth
  In Immanuel's land.

Oh! well it is for ever,
  Oh! well for evermore—
My nest hung in no forest
  Of all this death-doom'd shore;
Yea, let the vain world vanish,
  As from the ship the strand,
While glory—glory dwelleth
  In Immanuel's land.

There the Red Rose of Sharon
   Unfolds its heartmost bloom,
And fills the air of heaven
   With ravishing perfume:
Oh! to behold it blossom,
   While by its fragrance fann'd,
Where glory—glory dwelleth
   In Immanuel's land.

The King there in His beauty
   Without a veil is seen:
It were a well-spent journey,
   Though sev'n deaths lay between:
The Lamb, with His fair army,
   Doth on Mount Zion stand,
And glory—glory dwelleth
   In Immanuel's land.

Oh! Christ He is the fountain,
   The deep sweet well of love!
The streams on earth I've tasted,
   More deep I'll drink above:
There, to an ocean fulness,
   His mercy doth expand,
And glory—glory dwelleth
   In Immanuel's land.

Oft in yon sea-beat prison
   My Lord and I held tryst:
For Anwoth was not heaven,
   And preaching was not Christ;
And aye, my murkiest storm-cloud
   Was by a rainbow spann'd,
Caught from the glory dwelling
   In Immanuel's land.

But that He built a heaven
   Of His surpassing love—
A little New Jerusalem,
   Like to the one above:
"Lord, take me o'er the water,"
   Had been my loud demand,
"Take me to love's own country,
   Into Immanuel's land."

But flow'rs need night's cool darkness,
   The moonlight and the dew;
So Christ from one who loved it,
   His shining oft withdrew,
And then for cause of absence,
   My troubled soul I scanned—
But glory, shadeless, shineth
   In Immanuel's land.

The little birds of Anwoth,
   I used to count them blest,
Now, beside happier altars
   I go to build my nest;
O'er these there broods no silence,
   No graves around them stand,
For glory, deathless, dwelleth
   In Immanuel's land.

Fair Anwoth, by the Solway,
   To me thou still art dear!
E'en from the verge of heaven
   I drop for thee a tear.
Oh! if one soul from Anwoth
   Meet me at God's right hand,
My heaven will be two heavens
   In Immanuel's land.

I've wrestled on towards heaven,
  'Gainst storm, and wind, and tide;
Now, like a weary traveller,
  That leaneth on his guide,
Amid the shades of evening,
  While sinks life's lingering sand,
I hail the glory dawning
  From Immanuel's land.

Deep waters cross'd life's pathway,
  The hedge of thorns was sharp;
Now, these lie all behind me—
  Oh! for a well-tuned harp!
Oh! to join hallelujah
  With yon triumphant band,
Who sing, where glory dwelleth,
  In Immanuel's land.

With mercy and with judgment,
  My web of time He wove,
And aye, the dews of sorrow
  Were lustred with His love;
I'll bless the hand that guided,
  I'll bless the heart that plann'd,
When throned where glory dwelleth,
  In Immanuel's land.

Soon shall the cup of glory
  Wash down earth's bitt'rest woes;
Soon shall the desert briar
  Break into Eden's rose;
The curse shall change to blessing—
  The name on earth that's bann'd
Be graven on the white stone
  In Immanuel's land.

Oh! I am my Belovèd's,
  And my Beloved is mine!
He brings a poor vile sinner
  Into His "house of wine";
I stand upon His merit,
  I know no safer stand,
Not e'en where glory dwelleth,
  In Immanuel's land.

I shall sleep sound in Jesus,
  Fill'd with His likeness rise,
To love and to adore Him,
  To see Him with these eyes;
'Tween me and resurrection
  But Paradise doth stand;
Then—then for glory dwelling
  In Immanuel's land!

The bride eyes not her garment,
  But her dear Bridegroom's face;
I will not gaze at glory,
  But on my King of Grace—
Not at the crown He giveth,
  But on His piercèd hand:
The Lamb is all the glory
  Of Immanuel's land.

I have borne scorn and hatred,
  I have borne wrong and shame,
Earth's proud ones have reproached me
  For Christ's thrice blessèd name:
Where God's seals set the fairest,
  They've stamp'd their foulest brand,
But judgment shines like noonday
  In Immanuel's land.

They've summoned me before them,
   But there I may not come—
My Lord says, "Come up hither,"
   My Lord says, "Welcome home!"
My kingly King, on His white throne,
   My presence doth command,
Where glory—glory dwelleth
   In Immanuel's land.

NOTE.—SAMUEL RUTHERFORD, M.A., was a minister of the Gospel at Anworth [also spelled Anwoth—Ed.], Galloway, for many years. On July 26th, 1636, he was deprived by the High Commission Court of his ministry in the Kingdom of Scotland, and ordered to confinement within the City of Aberdeen during the King's pleasure. Here he remained for two years, when he ventured to return to Anworth. After a stormy life he died at St. Andrews in March 1661, just as he was about to undergo other trials in that cause to which his life had been so ardently devoted. The preceding verses are altogether composed of sentences, I believe, culled from his writings. They breathe such a spirit of joy and rest under trials and afflictions that their perusal can only delight the heart of the Christian, and encourage greatly those of the Lord's people who are specially tried.—COMPILER.

✢ PEACE ✢

IN a quiet hamlet an aged man was dying, and someone asking if he would like her to read to him some assuring gospel messages out of the Bible, he replied in his own broad Scotch dialect, "Na, na, lassie, I thacket [*thatched*] the hoose in calm weather, and it's no need't noo when the storms come on."

Happy man! Death was at the door; his faculties were failing; the earthly tabernacle was being taken down; the storm had come; but he was safely sheltered.

Little Tangles

ONCE upon a time there was a great king who employed his people to weave for him. The silk, and woof, and patterns were all given by the king, and he looked for diligent work-people. He was very indulgent, and told them when any difficulty arose to send to him, and he would help them, and never to fear troubling him, but to ask for help and instruction.

Among many men and women busy at their looms was one little child whom the king did not think too young to work. Often alone at her work, cheerfully and patiently she laboured. One day, when the men and women were distressed at the sight of their failures, the silks were tangled and the weaving unlike the pattern, they gathered round the child and said:

"Tell us how it is that you are so happy in your work. We are always in difficulties."

"Then why do you not send to the king?" said the little weaver; "he told us that we might do so."

"So we do, night and morning."

"Ah," said the child, "but I send **directly** I find I have a little tangle."

* * * * * *

We all have "little tangles" in our lives, and are discouraged because we cannot make them straight; so, instead of singing at our work, we are heavy-hearted and complaining. But is there **really** so easy a remedy always at hand? **May** we send **directly** to the King? Let us hear what He says about it Himself, for if it is true, why should we go on carrying all our burdens, and keeping all our sorrows pent up within?

"Cast thy burden upon the Lord, and He shall sustain thee." *Psalm 55:22.*

"Casting all your care upon Him; for He careth for you." *1 Peter 5:7.*

"Be careful for nothing; but in EVERYTHING, by prayer and supplication, with thanksgiving, let your requests be made known unto God." *Philippians 4:6.*

Every word of the Bible means what it says: "ALL"—"IN EVERYTHING"—mean just what they say. Then there is not a single thing shut out, from the smallest every-day care that worries to the greatest sorrow that nearly breaks the heart. Nor is the King, like earthly ones, difficult of access: "HIS EARS ARE OPEN TO THEIR CRY."

Though by seraph hosts adored, He to earth's lowest cares is still awake. And not only so, but He **comes** to us in our need, the call of a thought will bring Him close to our side.

Take, then, ye toiling and troubled ones, the comfort offered you; food is no use to the hungry, if they look at it, and do not eat; so you will be no happier or stronger if you only read the words of promised help; **act** upon them daily, hourly; go to the King **directly** you have a little tangle, "in **everything**," "**all** your care." Only take Him at His word, and you will find Him true to His word: "THE CROOKED PLACES WILL BE MADE STRAIGHT, AND THE ROUGH PLACES PLAIN," "AND THE PEACE OF GOD ... SHALL KEEP YOUR HEARTS AND MINDS THROUGH CHRIST JESUS."

❋ ❋ ❋

"But He giveth *more* grace"

IN clearing a flower bed the other day to make room for some fruit trees I learned a salutary lesson. The most difficult to pull up were the rose bushes, because they were more covered with thorns than any of the others. At the same time the rose was the sweetest flower that bloomed in the bed. There was a combination of the most thorns and the sweetest scent.

Ah! thought I, how like many a Christian. With some it is quite easy to be pleasant and amiable, and pleasantness and amiability may be mistaken for the graces of Christ. But when a rough, uncouth man is transformed into a gentle, lowly follower of Jesus, this is indeed grace. When a close, miserly person is generous and openhanded, this is indeed a triumph.

And of all the bushes and plants I rooted up the thorny rose was the one I was most careful to find a new place for.

May this little illustration be an encouragement to some of the Lord's people, who find it difficult to be pleasant and gracious, to think that if grace works in their hearts, the Lord may find His sweetest roses upon His thorniest bushes. We are apt to judge superficially, and see much grace where there is little, and little where there is much. God reads aright, and values the flowers of His own cultivation.

James and John afford a good example of what I mean. The Lord surnamed them "Boanerges," or "Sons of Thunder." From that, and the fact that they united in asking the Lord to command fire to consume the village of the Samaritans, who refused them, we gather that they were rough, impatient, noisy men. Their mother was ambitious, too, in asking for her sons the chief places in the kingdom, and such a mother was likely to have ambitious sons. The fact that they accompanied her when the request was made seems to point to this very clearly.

But see how grace worked. From the Acts of the Apostles we gather that James had developed into a man, content rather to suffer martyrdom for Christ's sake, with no trace of the Boanerges about him. John from his writings is seen to be gentle, tender, deeply affectionate—he had well graduated from the top place in the Lord's school—his head upon his Master's breast—certainly the Boanerges had been rooted out of him, the lion of nature had given place to the lamb of grace.

God ... the Great Deliverer

How often have the words of the Psalmist King charmed us:—

"I have been young, and now am old; yet have I not seen the righteous forsaken, nor his seed begging bread."

(*Psalm 37:25*),

and how often have the deliverances recorded in Scripture found a present-day illustration in our own lives or under our own observation?

The Bible teems with deliverances and is pregnant with hope. Not always does God deliver out of trials, but He always carries His people through them, and gives them hope. But God often delivers; indeed, in some cases (we say it reverently) He must, because of His own character.

It is when circumstances close around us and leave no possible way of escape unless God makes it that deliverance is sure to come. What escape was possible to the Israelites when the Egyptians pursued them? None, absolutely none, humanly speaking. How often we have sung,

> "Thine arm hath safely brought us
> A way no more expected,
> Than when Thy sheep passed through the deep
> By crystal walls protected."

Again, only God could have made a way of escape for the three Hebrew children. Who would have thought of the fire burning their bands and slaying their enemies and giving them the company of the Son of God in such a special fashion?

Again, only God could have made a way of escape for Daniel in the den of lions. Only God could have shut their mouths and used them as a bodyguard for His servant instead of devouring him. They were hungry enough, as Daniel's enemies soon found out when they themselves were thrown into the den.

What need to multiply instances? The Bible teems with them. The Apostle Paul's life was made up of deliverances when he wrote of God those grateful and triumphant words:—

"Who delivered us from so great a death, and doth deliver: in whom we trust that He will yet deliver."

(2 Corinthians 1:10).

Past, present and future! What a God! How we can trust Him.

Two instances come to my mind as happening under my own observation.

An old Christian lady sitting in her armchair. Her aged husband, an invalid, on the sofa. The last piece of food taken from the shelf and eaten, and the last shovelful of coal burning out on the hearth. Yet her spirit was brave, and her trust, deepened by many an experience, strong as ever. Her husband grew petulant, and wanted to know what was to be done. "God will provide," she calmly replied, and his impatient rejoinder was cut short by a knock at the door. A Christian lady handed in an envelope with the message that her mother could not rest till it was brought. The envelope contained a five-pound note. The aged husband burst into tears when he saw how God had answered his wife's faith.

A Christian young man was in need of work. Most industriously he looked for it, and wore out two or three pairs of boots in its search. Meanwhile he was living on a small sum of money realised by the sale of an aunt's furniture. Smaller and smaller it dwindled, till at length the last shilling was spent and hope of work seemed as far off as ever. A Christian, who had taken a deep interest in his case, gave him a sovereign (which he could not well spare), but before it was spent work was found most unexpectedly; and from that day to this, an interval of several years, he has not wanted health or work.

I have often noticed that it is when the circumstances are hopeless as far as men are concerned God comes in.

"God is faithful, who will not suffer you to be tempted above that ye are able; but will with the temptation also make a way to escape, that ye may be able to bear it."

(1 Corinthians 10:13).

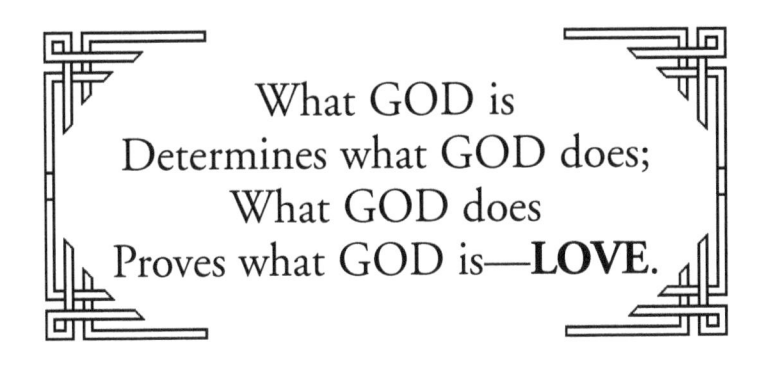

> What GOD is
> Determines what GOD does;
> What GOD does
> Proves what GOD is—**LOVE**.

Simply Clinging

"HE took them up in His arms, put His hands upon them, and blessed them." *Mark 10:16.*

This is what He does where there is no conscious strength, but simple clinging. It is more than turning to His power or His mercy; it is simple repose in the arms of Christ. It just lies there, and has the satisfaction of being taken care of. Here, then, I get CONFIDENCE. I feel that I simply could not do without the Lord. Is it not pleasant for the heart to be able thus to delight in God?—to be able to say: I am a poor creature, without means, but He has taken me up in His arms, laid His hands upon me, and blessed me; whereas, if I were a man of great natural resources, perhaps I should find it very difficult to give up everything for Christ.